# Education Write Now

In this innovative new series *Education Write Now*, ten of education's most inspiring thought-leaders meet for a three-day retreat to think and write collaboratively, and then bring you the top takeaways you need right now to improve your school or classroom. This first volume, edited by Jeffrey Zoul and Joe Mazza, focuses on the all-important, but often uncomfortable, concept of change. Each concise chapter addresses how teachers and leaders can do the hard work of enacting change so more students succeed—academically and emotionally.

You'll gain practical insights and strategies for changing how we think about . . .

- Embracing Change (Jeffrey Zoul)
- Learning (Tony Sinanis)
- Assessment (Starr Sackstein)
- Relationships (Kayla Delzer)
- Mental Health (Joe Mazza)
- Educational Technology (Thomas Murray)
- Teacher Engagement (Sanée Bell)
- Leadership (Amber Teamann)
- Partnerships (Bob Dillon)
- Communication (Joe Sanfelippo)

The royalties generated from this book will support the Will To Live Foundation, a nonprofit foundation working to prevent teen suicide.

**Dr. Jeffrey Zoul** (@jeff_zoul) is a lifelong teacher, learner, and leader. During Jeff's distinguished career in education he has served in a variety of roles, most recently as Assistant Superintendent for Teaching and Learning with Deerfield Public Schools District 109 in Illinois. Jeff also served as a teacher and coach in Georgia before moving into school administration. He has authored many books, including *What Connected Educators Do Differently*.

**Dr. Joe Mazza** (@joe_mazza) is Lecturer at The University of Pennsylvania's Graduate School of Education. He is the Founder/CEO of MakerDads, a new father and family engagement initiative bringing dads, grand-dads, and other male role models together to support student learning through innovation. Joe's innovative work has been featured in 15 books dating back to 2005. Most recently, he co-authored *Lead Learners: Creating a Culture of Empathy, Innovation, and Empowerment* with Derek McCoy (Routledge, 2018).

## *Also Available From Routledge*
## *Eye On Education*
(www.routledge.com/eyeoneducation)

**What Connected Educators Do Differently**
Todd Whitaker, Jeffrey Zoul, Jimmy Casas

**Intentional Innovation:**
**How to Guide Risk-Taking, Build Creative Capacity,**
**and Lead Change**
A.J. Juliani

**Inquiry and Innovation in the Classroom:**
**Using 20% Time, Genius Hour, and PBL**
**to Drive Student Success**
A.J. Juliani

**The Passion-Driven Classroom, 2nd Edition:**
**A Framework for Teaching and Learning**
Angela Maiers and Amy Sandvold

**The Genius Hour Guidebook:**
**Fostering Passion, Wonder, and Inquiry in the Classroom**
Denise Krebs and Gallit Zvi

**Passionate Learners, 2nd Edition:**
**How to Engage and Empower Your Students**
Pernille Ripp

**Passionate Readers:**
**The Art of Reaching and Engaging Every Child**
Pernille Ripp

**What Great Teachers Do Differently, 2nd Edition:**
**17 Things That Matter Most**
Todd Whitaker

**Your First Year:**
**How to Survive and Thrive as a New Teacher**
Todd Whitaker, Madeline Whitaker, Katherine Whitaker

# Education Write Now

Edited by Jeffrey Zoul and Joe Mazza

Routledge
Taylor & Francis Group

NEW YORK AND LONDON

First published 2018
by Routledge
711 Third Avenue, New York, NY 10017

and by Routledge
2 Park Square, Milton Park, Abingdon, Oxon, OX14 4RN

*Routledge is an imprint of the Taylor & Francis Group, an informa business*

*Library of Congress Cataloging-in-Publication Data*
A catalog record has been requested

ISBN: 978-1-138-29637-4 (pbk)
ISBN: 978-1-315-14812-0 (ebk)

Typeset in Palatino
by Apex CoVantage, LLC

The authors of this book would like to dedicate this project to the many people impacted by suicide, including friends and family members who continue to ache from their losses. In addition, each author has begun his/her chapter with a personal dedication to someone who has taken his or her own life or has been affected by such a tragedy. Proceeds from this book go to the Will To Live Foundation, a nonprofit organization focused on preventing teen suicide. The organization works to improve the lives and the "Will To Live" of teenagers everywhere through education about mental health and encouraging them to recognize the love and hope that exist in each other.

# Contents

# Meet the Editors

**Dr. Jeffrey Zoul** is a lifelong teacher, learner, and leader. During Jeff's distinguished career in education he has served in a variety of roles, most recently as Assistant Superintendent for Teaching and Learning with Deerfield Public Schools District 109 in Deerfield, Illinois. Jeff also served as a teacher and coach in the State of  Georgia for many years before moving into school administration. Jeff has taught graduate courses at the university level in the areas of assessment, research, and program evaluation. He is the author/co-author of many books, including *What Connected Educators Do Differently; Start. Right. Now.—Teach and Lead for Excellence; Improving Your School One Week at a Time;* and *Leading Professional Learning: Tools to Connect and Empower Teachers.* Jeff has earned several degrees, including his undergraduate degree from the University of Massachusetts and his doctoral degree from the University of Alabama. In his spare time, Jeff enjoys running and has completed over a dozen marathons. You can follow Jeff's blog at jeffreyzoul@blogspot.com or connect with him on Twitter @jeff_zoul.

**Dr. Joe Mazza** is a father, learner, and creative educator who spurs innovation across UPenn's Mid-Career Doctoral Program in Educational Leadership (@MCDPEL). Aside from Mazza's teaching responsibilities at UPenn, he is Founder/CEO of Mak-erDads, a new traveling father and family and community engagement

mobile makerspace. He is a frequent speaker, blogger, and podcaster both in the U.S. and internationally on family, community, and school partnerships, as well as innovative leadership and technology integration for personal and professional growth. Joe is a strong relationship builder and communicator committed to on-demand learning and ensuring students, educators, and parents understand the power of utilizing networks throughout the learning process. He is co-author with Derek McCoy of *Lead Learners: Creating a Culture of Empathy, Innovation, and Empowerment*. In his spare time, Joe enjoys retro video games, "making" at home with his four children, and cheering on his alma mater, Penn State, at Beaver Stadium each fall. You can follow Joe's blog at medium.com/@joe_mazza or connect with him on Twitter @joe_mazza.

# Introduction

When I was a sixth-grade teacher, I felt alone at times. Sure, I had 100 amazing, excited, hyper middle school students, but I lacked peers. I longed for adult connections.

The principal meant well and assigned me a mentor, but the mentor was always too busy to meet. My colleague down the hall was happy to help me and share her worksheets . . . but that wasn't how I wanted to teach.

A lot of people know this feeling all too well. Teaching can be a lonely profession. Maybe it's because you spend so much time in your room and not enough time visiting other classrooms. Maybe it's because you care so darn much about your kids and can't always help them as much as you'd like. Maybe it's the lack of support from people who think teachers have it easy because they have summers off, when you're pouring your blood and sweat into your work. But you go on, because you care.

Just as teachers can feel isolated, so can building leaders. The principal can get the blame for everything that goes wrong. Even when things go right, there is a sense of separation and intimidation. The principal walks into a room and people act fake because it is their boss. It's lonely at the top.

For those of us who stay in education, we brush the bad parts aside. We forge ahead because we care so much. We want to succeed.

But what if we don't hide the bad parts quite so much? What if we find a way to be more honest with ourselves? What if we embrace our struggles, our vulnerability, and our humanness, in our classrooms and hallways, so we can deepen our connections and feel less alone? What if we take time away from the testing and routines to remember our purpose? What if we admit that learning—and life—can be messy, frightening, and hard? How would that help us personally, with colleagues, and in our roles?

And how would it help us reach students on a deeper, more personalized level so we can model the way for them?

Kids *need* us to be real, now more than ever. Anxiety and depression have been on the rise among high school students, and we can't afford to ignore that (Schrobsdorff, 2016). We need to make a change. We need to adjust how we reach them, and we need to change education so we can teach students more deeply, preparing them for a new kind of future, one most of us can't imagine.

And that's where this book comes in.

This book is about changing education right now, but you can't enact change if you don't dig deep and look inside yourself. So while each chapter addresses a different aspect of change at the classroom and building levels, you'll notice there's an undercurrent about being vulnerable, being personal, being real—and treating each and every student as an individual.

Jeff Zoul begins by tackling the big picture issue of **what change actually entails**. He admits how he resisted change so fiercely when he stepped into a new leadership role and what he learned from that. He explains what change means and how we can get others on board to truly make a difference.

Tony Sinanis then reveals the first thing we need to change in education—our approach to the learning itself. We need to **change how we think about learning in the classroom and learning for teachers and staff**. It's not enough to say we want to create a community of life-long learners; we need to reflect on what that means and how we can achieve it. The learning process is not meant to be easy—it should be personalized, it should be messy, and it should help students for the rest of their lives.

Kayla Delzer builds on this discussion of personalized learning and takes us into the classroom. She asks us to **change how we think about our relationships with students** and their families. It's not enough to do an icebreaker activity the first day and then jump into the content. We need to foster a deep relationship with each student—and his or her family—before we can expect learning to happen in a meaningful way.

Starr Sackstein also asks us to think of the individual. In her chapter on **changing how we approach assessment**, she reminds us that a student should not be defined by a grade. We might be confined by state exams and grades, but we can teach students how to value the learning and embrace failures. If students self-assess and self-reflect in deeper ways, they'll have the skills they need to grow throughout life.

Thomas C. Murray adds to the conversation about reaching students and shows us that we're not truly teaching them if we're just throwing the latest tech tools and fads their way. In his chapter on **changing our approach to technology in schools**, he reminds us that it's not about the device or the latest trend. It's about using tools to reach objectives and teach students to be creative problem solvers. That is what they need to face challenges in their futures, beyond school doors.

Joe Mazza steps in to remind us that on this journey to help students learn, we can't ignore mental health issues. He urges us to **change how we think about mental health**, and he encourages us to be brave and discuss our own life challenges with students and colleagues when appropriate. This can help students with their own mental health issues, which have been on the rise. Joe shows how we can support students and how we can improve our own mental health by being vulnerable and forging connections with others. These connections will help us personally and will help us engage more deeply in our work.

Sanée Bell builds on this idea of deeper connections and engagement, encouraging leaders to **change how they engage teachers**. Teachers might comply and do their jobs, but that is not enough. We often hear strategies for fostering student ownership in the classroom, but what about teachers? How can leaders give teachers ownership in their roles, too, so they feel like co-creators in the school's mission and keep their passion alive?

Amber Teamann continues the discussion of a leader's position. School leaders make administrative decisions and put out fires daily, but they also play a key role in the culture of the school. Amber asks us to **change how we approach leadership** by taking the time to think about our emotional intelligence (EI).

If we use EI and relational leadership, we can foster a better environment for students, teachers, and families.

Bob Dillon extends the conversation beyond the building level and reminds us that schools do not exist on their own. Bob asks us to **change how we think about partnerships**. What does it mean to partner with schools in a way that creates a genuine, modern community around students and adult learners? How can we use apprenticeships, arts integration, communities by design, restorative justice, and other methods to connect schools and communities?

And finally, Joe Sanfelippo reminds us that we need to **change the narrative of how schools are talked about**. We can do the hard work in our schools, but the sad truth is that education can be undervalued and underappreciated in society. How can we celebrate our successes to improve our communities and foster learning and citizenship on a larger scale?

We hope that each chapter gives you ideas, strategies, and inspiration to help you on your journey toward real change in your school or classroom. And we hope it also gives you the courage to be vulnerable, because change involves risk and you can't make a difference if you don't put yourself out there.

As you read the pages that follow, you'll see that the authors featured are not just preaching vulnerability; they're embracing it by being honest about their own struggles. In their chapters, they share what they did wrong as teachers or leaders before they made a change. They're also being vulnerable by embracing the writing process together. They wrote this book in person, during a writing retreat, one that we hope will happen annually and produce a new volume each year. These authors are all extremely respected educators with amazing ideas to offer, but they realize that sometimes you can't write or create in isolation. They wanted to get together in person to learn from one another and push one another, because sometimes you need to share ideas and collaborate and peer edit the way we ask our students to do. We enjoyed the experience of meeting, reflecting, and sharing, and we hope that the book inspires you to learn and connect with students and colleagues on your own journey. When we learn and connect as individuals with a shared purpose, we're one step closer to making real changes and improving education, right now.

—Lauren Davis
Routledge

## Reference

Schrobsdorff, Susanna, (2016, October). Teen Depression and Anxiety: Why the Kids Are Not Alright. TIME, Retrieved from http://time.com/magazine/us/4547305/november-7th-2016-vol-188-no-19-u-s/

## Join the Conversation

Want to continue the discussion about the ideas in this book? Tweet using the hashtag #EdWriteNow. We would love to hear from you. We'd also love to hear your ideas for next year's book!

## Our Cause

The royalties from this book will go to the Will To Live Foundation, a suicide-prevention organization that educates students to lean on one another and get help for their friends in need. We've all been affected by suicide and we begin each chapter with a dedication to someone we've lost or someone we know who has been affected.

# 1

# Changing the Way We Think About Change

## Jeffrey Zoul

This chapter is dedicated to the memory of Mike, a former colleague and trusted friend.

## A Short Story of Simple Change

Exactly four years ago from the date I am writing these words, I changed school districts, moving from a district office administrative position in one community to a similar position a few hours away. As with most job changes, the move was bittersweet: I absolutely loved the previous community I served, yet was equally enthusiastic about my new position and the people with whom I would be serving. When I arrived for my first day of work at the new district, one of the first things I learned was that they had recently become a "Google Apps for Education" district. As such, the email platform for all employees was Gmail and the default vehicle for creating standard documents was Google Docs. Although it seems almost impossible to believe four years hence, at the time I had no idea what this meant. I came from a district that used Microsoft Outlook and Microsoft Word. To say I was less than receptive to this sudden change in my work habits would be quite an understatement; in fact, I was openly rebellious to the idea. A great deal of my daily work routine included writing and responding to emails and creating written documents of various kinds to share with various stakeholders. For these important tasks, which consumed several hours of my every workday, Outlook and Word had served me well and had never presented me with any problems. In fact, I could not imagine a better way to do either of these tasks. In this case, the old adage "If it ain't broke, don't fix it" resonated with me and—although I am embarrassed to admit it now—I freely shared my pointed opinion with anyone in my new school district who would listen. I even tried to sabotage the change-over to these new platforms, suggesting that we allow people choice between the two, since I soon learned I was but one of many opposed to this change. Luckily for me—and for every student and staff member in our district—wiser heads prevailed and we stuck with the decision to change. In just a few days, I was starting to understand the "new" email platform and even realize some of its advantages over my previous tool. Not long after, the same occurred with my transition to Google Docs, as I became comfortable with how it worked and discovered the huge potential for collaboration it offered. After working for a full month with these two new tools, I, of course, never looked back, using them effectively and efficiently, learning more about them with each passing day, and fully understanding why this change had been effected.

This short story of simple change—although, admittedly, a relatively mundane one—still stands out in my memory as typical of many other changes we undergo. Although some of us are more comfortable with change than others, I suspect that we all have stories about being faced with some sort of change and responding—at least, initially—with some level of resistance. And, while my own story of change is a rather small one compared to some larger-scale change initiatives I have witnessed in education during my thirty-five years in public schools, I think it is an important reminder about what I once thought and what I now think. It is also fair to point out that I am sharing a change success story; I have also experienced change initiatives that failed miserably. Although we can, and should, learn from our failures in life—including any change initiatives we have experienced that have not worked out as planned—it might behoove us to start with success stories when changing the way we think about change, seeking answers to these and other questions:

- ◆ What went right?
- ◆ How did we overcome the obstacles to change?
- ◆ How did people initially respond, both the trailblazers and the saboteurs?
- ◆ Why did we decide to pursue change in the first place?
- ◆ How did we support affected stakeholders throughout the change process?
- ◆ What were the benefits of the change, once fully implemented?
- ◆ What, if anything, was better about the previous model and how did we address this?

I could go on. In education, some amount of change is ever present, as we continuously reflect, seeking ongoing improvements and determining the necessary changes we must make to improve. I suspect our industry is not unique in this respect, of course. I doubt there exists a successful business, medical practice, law office, or athletic team that is not constantly trying to improve and changing the way they do things in order to get better at what they do. Although all organizations experience changes in the way they do things, at times I fear that education—even with all the changes we have seen over time— has undergone less dramatic, transformational change than other industries. In fact, to draw on another familiar adage, when it comes to public education in our great nation, it sometimes strikes me that "the more things change, the more they remain the same." Something tells me, however, that our noble profession is facing a tipping point when it comes to change. Now is the time for real change, change that moves beyond using one email platform or another; change that goes beyond moving from interactive whiteboards to some other projection system; change that truly reimagines the way in which we evaluate our individual and collective performance; change that requires us to actually stop doing some things completely. In education, the time for change is now, regardless of our comfort level with this premise. There have been sputtering calls for education "reform" over the years. Then, we "changed" our tune, suggesting that rather than "reforming" education, we must "transform" education. I completely understand and support this subtle distinction. Wagner et al. (Wagner et al., 2006) make the compelling case: "Education reform" implies that at some point in the past, our education system was just fine and all we need do is make minor improvements to return to this era of success. Even if we accept the premise that our educational system was just fine at some point in the past, the fact remains that our nation's needs have changed since that time, our nation's demographics have changed since that time, our career pathways have changed since that time, our children have changed since that time, our family structures have changed since that time, and resources available to us have changed since that time. The time for "reform" has long since passed us by; the time to transform is now—before this concept, too, becomes yet another educational buzzword that results only in finding better ways of doing the same old thing. Rather than asking how we can simply function more *effectively*, we must ask ourselves how we must function *differently*. Doing things better is good. Doing better things is even better. In education, we always have and always will strive to do things better. The time is now, however, to do better things. The future of our country—every student in every classroom—demands that we act and act now.

## Good Enough Is Not Good Enough

"If it ain't broke, don't fix it." I have to admit that years ago this was almost a mantra of mine. Moreover, even today the sentiment behind the saying still makes perfect sense to me: why would we want to change something that works? Like seemingly everything in education, I see both sides of this argument. For better or for worse, our profession is much more gray than black and white. Reflecting on this question, two answers immediately jump to mind. First, when we say it currently works, the cynic in me pauses to ask, "For whom? Is it working for everyone? Is it working for students? For adults? How do we know it is working? What are the success metrics?" Second, and perhaps even more important: Are we settling for "good enough" when, in fact, there may be a whole new level of success to enjoy if only we changed our thoughts and our actions? How long should we continue using the same programs, tools, techniques, and methods because they "work" and we are getting "good" results?

For far too long in this great nation, our public education system has been settling for "good enough." As Collins suggested (Collins, 2001) the reason we have so few great schools is because we have so many good schools. Our kids deserve better than "good enough" and so do we, as educators. My first car (a 1971 Volkswagen Karmann Ghia) worked (usually) well in getting me from Point A to Point B. My current vehicle, however, makes that one look like an antiquated relic. Moreover, we are about to experience an even larger leap forward in automobile technology, with gas-powered vehicles becoming a thing of the past (as I write these words, Volvo just announced that after 2019 they will cease production of automobiles powered solely by gasoline) and automated driving assistance technology becoming the norm. The medical profession is undergoing transformational changes as well. In 1858, Douglas Bly invented and patented an early version of a prosthetic limb. Today, experts are using 3D printing technology to revolutionize the way we make prosthetic limbs. The way we communicate has experienced revolutionary change: my first flip phone worked well, at least for making phone calls. Today's "cell phones" can do that and a whole lot more. In the fourteen years that have passed from my first such device to the one I use today, the capabilities of this tool have been radically altered for the better. In each of these instances, we could have settled for "good enough." Thankfully, generations of dreamers and doers decided that good enough wasn't good enough, demanding, defining, and creating a better way. They moved from merely improving the status quo to inventing a completely different way to do what was previously done. Radical improvement requires radical change. As an educator, I am proud of some changes we have made to improve our status quo, yet I know we have not changed enough. Our schools are good. I have visited public schools in at least forty of our fifty states. In each, the schools I visited were good. They were filled with hardworking students and staff who cared about what they were doing and with whom they were doing it. You might say that these schools were all "good enough," yet much of what I saw resembled the classrooms I learned in myself more than forty years ago. Despite minor changes, these spaces were similar to what they were decades earlier and that is no longer acceptable. Where is education's version of driverless cars, 3D created prosthetic limbs, and transferring the entire body of available knowledge from large libraries to small devices in our pockets? And how can we change our thinking to make it happen?

## Changing Our Thinking

"Change your thoughts and you change your world" is a quote often attributed to Norman Vincent Peale. Making changes to the status quo is often fraught with challenges along the way and, perhaps as a result, it seems we talk a whole lot more about changing than actually changing anything we currently do. Although it is critically important that we move from *talking* about transformational change to *acting* upon transformational change initiatives, the change process starts with each of us as individuals, specifically, with the thoughts we each have about what needs changing, why it must change, and how we can make change happen. It seems an oversimplified notion to believe that if we merely change the way we think about things, we can change our entire world, but the power of a growth mindset open to change cannot be overstated. We begin to change ourselves, our world, and the world around us when we intentionally make the time to reflect on what we are doing and whether our actions are having the desired impact.

In looking back over my many years in education and the changes in my own thinking about teaching, learning, and leading during that time, it is almost alarming to consider the extent to which I have altered my views. Moreover, when I consider the opinions I used to hold as truths, I also recall how strongly I believed in them. I was convinced I was right about things then that I feel completely different about now. Of course, I must continue the ongoing process of reflecting because what I am certain I am right about today is likely (hopefully?) going to change yet again years hence. If you have been an educator for ten years or more, what are some thoughts you had about our profession when you started that have changed dramatically over time? Doing a bit of honest—and somewhat embarrassing—reflection, here is just a sample of what I used to think and what I now think:

- ◆ I used to think . . . that students should be held to high standards of personal behavior and that we should administer rigid and harsh consequences including long-term out-of-school suspensions when they misbehaved. Now I think . . . that students should be held to high standards of personal behavior and we should teach them what that looks like and how it enhances their lives. And when they misbehave (which they will), I think we should keep them in school, helping them to understand why the behavior in question was detrimental to themselves and/or others and working with them to behave differently in the future. Punishing students who misbehaved typically resulted in the same students misbehaving again; even though it rarely worked, I still did it. I think differently about this important issue now than I used to.
- ◆ I used to think . . . that due dates were set in stone and that everything I assigned must be turned in on the day it was due with no exceptions. Now I think . . . that I was letting students off the hook by giving them zeroes for work not completed by the "due date." Now I think that the natural consequence for someone not doing the assigned work by the prescribed due date is for them to still complete and turn in the assignment. The many zeroes I so righteously assigned to students who missed due dates rarely, if ever, changed such students' subsequent efforts

and no learning occurred once the zero was entered into my gradebook. I think differently about this important issue now than I used to.

- ◆ I used to think . . . that when hiring new staff or filling slots on our school leadership teams, I should seek like-minded professionals who thought like I did and shared many of my same attributes and skillsets. Now I think . . . that when hiring new staff or determining who should sit on leadership teams, I should seek out people who complement my own skills and who are willing to honestly disagree and push back on my ideas when they think these ideas are not best for kids. Ideally, I select colleagues who are different from me in as many ways as possible, but sharing in common the goal to do what is best for the kids we serve. When I surrounded myself with people just like me, I rarely grew as an individual and the school I served was limited in terms of how far we could take it since our perspectives were limited. I think differently about this important issue now than I used to.

These are but three startling changes in my own thinking I have had over the years; again, I could go on. Some of the thoughts and beliefs I previously adhered to are ones that now, quite honestly, make me cringe. As I write these words, reflecting upon these thoughts and others I held fast to and have now relinquished for newer, better, and completely different thoughts, I am both thankful for the change in my thinking as well as somewhat ashamed I ever had such professional opinions. Here is the thing, though: like almost every single educator I have ever known, I was doing what I thought was best at that point in time. As we often say, very few educators wake up in the morning thinking, "I'd like to be entirely mediocre today." Instead, they arise each morning with the honest intention to bring their "A" game that day, just like they did the day before. So it is with our thoughts. The thoughts I had then were based on what I was taught by others at the time and on the experiences I had as a student myself. I held these thoughts not because of a character flaw, laziness, or a desire to engage in professional malpractice; instead,

I thought this way because, at the time, the world of school I lived in convinced me this was best for kids. As hard as it is to comprehend that punishing kids and assigning them zeroes was best for them, that is, actually, why I did such things: at the time, I thought it was best for kids. Thankfully, over time, I changed my actions relating to student behavior, grading, and personnel; however, my actions changed only after giving the ideas many long hours, days, months, and years of thought, both alone and in collaboration with my colleagues. Eventually, my thoughts changed, which, in turn, changed my actions. Truly, changing our world starts with changing our thoughts. As a result, we must intentionally build time into our hectic professional lives to reflect on what we are doing and examining our thoughts about best practices. Then, we must change. Perhaps my favorite quote ever is this, from Maya Angelou: "Do the best you can until you know better. Then, when you know better, do better." There is no shame in having held a thought that was wrongheaded and even acting according to that thought. The only shame lies in not changing once you learn a better way.

## Change That Sticks

Why do some change efforts take root while others fizzle out over time? Although it was a first-order change of relatively small proportion, let's revisit my change from Word and Outlook to Gmail and Google Docs. First, I cannot overemphasize how much this change improved my professional life. Again, nothing against the tools I previously used; in fact, they served me well for many, many years and even today I know many smart and talented friends who use these tools and are highly productive people. But for me, this change that I initially resisted quite vociferously (and just a bit obnoxiously, I fear) ultimately transformed in a positive way certain aspects of my work. For me, the email features of the system I feared and fought against proved vastly superior to those available in the platform which I had been loathe to discard. My change in word processing tools was even more impactful. I fought this change even harder, yet soon found the benefits even more life enhancing than those associated with the change in email systems. In an extremely short time span, I went from being angry that I would no longer have access to Microsoft Word to being angry whenever I received (less and less frequently) an attachment that was in Word document form. I suddenly became irritated when someone used a software program that I, myself, had used and advocated for mere weeks earlier. (Side note: I clearly have anger issues; the goal when changing must not be about changing what you are angry about!) Seriously, though, I suspect this short story of simple change is not unlike those many readers may have experienced: 1. At some point, we are directed, rather than invited, to change something that currently works well for us. 2. We reluctantly accept the fact that we must change, even though we may resist and try to change the minds of those thrusting the change upon us. 3. Once we accept that we must change and commit to the change, we actually change our thoughts, change our actions, and discover that the change was beneficial.

So what can we learn about change and how to initiate change successfully from my short story of simple change? Let me suggest six important points to consider when implementing change in our classrooms, schools, and districts:

### Six Drivers of Successful CHANGE

**C:** *Clarify* In order to effect successful change in our schools, we must establish clarity of vision. As change agents, we must explicitly spell out why we are changing and what we hope to accomplish by changing. We must paint the picture of what the change process will look like and the results we hope to see when fully implemented. We must pose the question, "How will this change to the status quo impact our classroom/school/district for the better?" and continuously revisit the question to see if our initial compelling answers are being realized. In my short story of simple change, the change was successful, in part, because the leaders of the movement painted the picture of how my life would be better (albeit in a relatively small way) if I changed. For example, they explained how collaboration with colleagues would become more efficient and productive using Google Docs and that I would have unlimited storage with Gmail. Once forced to change, I soon learned the clear vision they had for increased productivity in our district was accurate.

**H**: *Help* In order to effect successful change in our schools, we must provide the help, support, and resources necessary, particularly when the change is directive, rather than invitational. We must plan in advance how we will help the entire organization adapt to the change as well as prepare for how we will differentiate support for individuals whose success moving from the status quo to the desired state deviates from the anticipated plan. We must pose the question, "How can we help the organization as a whole and each individual within the organization adapt to the change with as little disruption to their productivity and comfort as possible during the process?" and continuously revisit the question to see if our initial carefully thought-out answers are being realized. In my short story of simple change, the change was successful, in part, because there were people I could reach out to immediately when I had questions or experienced problems related to the new tools we were required to use. Those leading the change were available, patient, and helpful.

**A**: *Act* In order to effect successful change in our schools, we must establish a sense of urgency for the need to change and then act accordingly. There is a time for talk and a time for action. Too often when it comes to change, there is too much talk and too little action. Moreover, although it may well be appropriate to enact optional change initiatives in some instances, in many others it is necessary to mandate change. Using the word "mandate" often rubs us the wrong way as collaborative educators, but just as we would not withhold an educational service or intervention to a child who needs it even if they did not want it, we must also not allow individuals to opt out of change that is best for the organization and, ultimately, for them as members of the organization. We must pose the question, "When will our change initiative occur and how will we ensure that all members of the team are committing to the change?" and continuously revisit the question to see if our initial plan of action is being implemented as designed. In my short story of simple change, the change was successful, in part, because I was forced to act. When I asked for permission to opt out, I was told (politely and respectfully), "Nope." Had I not been directed to change, I likely would not have done so. My performance would have stagnated and I would have been acting in a way counterproductive to the goals of the district I served.

**N**: *Navigate* In order to effect successful change in our schools, we must proactively anticipate the obstacles we are likely to face and carefully navigate these as they arise. We must be prepared to stomp out fires swiftly, not allowing these inevitable bumps along the road from status quo to desired state to distract us from the ultimate destination. We must realize that some of these "obstacles" may be people on the team who are so opposed to the change that they will actively work against it. We must have a plan for working with these human obstacles, too, so that eventually, they either join the effort . . . or perhaps find a new organization more aligned with their own values. We must pose the question, "How will we respond when problems arise relating to the change initiative?" and continuously revisit the question to see if we are overcoming obstacles, including those we anticipated as well as those we did not. In my short story of simple change, the change was successful, in part, because a team from across the district met regularly well in advance of the change implementation to plan for every step of the journey. When problems arose, there was a sense of calm confidence that led those of us on the fence to become more confident that the change would be successful.

**G**: *Generate* In order to effect successful change in our schools, we must generate momentum and keep that momentum going until the change takes root organically throughout the organization. We must generate small wins, finding ways to celebrate successes along the way. We must generate increasing levels of support along the way, identifying people on the team who are enjoying success with the change initiative and enlisting these people to help in replicating this success with their colleagues. We must pose the question, "How will we recognize intermediate successes along our change journey and how will we celebrate these throughout the organization?" and continuously revisit the question to see if we are making the progress we had anticipated and making time to acknowledge such progress. In my short story of simple change, the change was successful, in part, because people with more expertise than I took the time to encourage me when I tried something new and it worked. These leaders in our district also asked teachers who were ahead of some of us to lead informal classes, sharing what they had been able to do with the new tools available to them and how it was positively impacting their teaching and, ultimately, student learning.

E: *Evaluate* In order to effect successful change in our schools, we must identify success metrics and schedule periodic measurements along the way to gauge what impact the change is having. Too often we enact a change and simply move forward, eventually deciding to either stay the course or revert back to the status quo, but with no real metrics driving the decision. People will be more receptive to change when they see results, including quantitative data as well as anecdotal stories. We must pose the question, "How will we know if the change initiative is making a positive difference in our school community?" and continuously revisit the question to see if our expected results are happening and determining how to respond when they are not. In my short story of simple change, the change was successful, in part, because members of the team leading the change periodically surveyed staff and shared those responses—which showed increasing levels of satisfaction over time with the new tools—with every staff member in the district.

Change is hard. Change can be scary. Change can be disruptive. Change can make us feel less safe. Change can force us to take one step forward and two steps back. Yet, if the change is better for those we serve, we must change. To increase our chances of effecting change successfully, we must *Clarify*, *Help*, *Act*, *Navigate*, *Generate*, and *Evaluate*.

## A Time for CHANGE

Over a year ago, a friend and I had an idea for changing the way we would write our next book. Instead of taking a year or more to write an individual full-length book in our typical solitary manner, we would invite eight other friends to gather for a weekend and spontaneously write a collaborative full-length book about important issues in education. This piece on the topic of change is my contribution to the project we envisioned back then and eventually brought to fruition. When we first hatched the concept, I had no idea I would be writing about "changing the way we think about change" in education. Now that I have, I realize that this project itself is one example of the change we need in education, change that totally reimagines the way we have traditionally done our work.

During our collaboration on this project, we spent most of the time writing, but we also talked, shared, debated, and provided feedback. When asking one of these writing partners for help in closing my piece on change, she suggested that public education needs to evolve, changing over time into a totally different institution. At first this made perfect sense, particularly since it came from one of the most intelligent thinkers I know. Upon further reflection, however, I question if this will ever happen. If public education should naturally evolve over time, changing into a transformed model of teaching, learning, and leading, would it not have happened by now? It should have, yet it has not. Evolution connotes gradual and continuous development until something changes from one stage to another. Despite the gradual and continuous changes that have impacted education over the past 100 years or more, we have yet to see a transformational shift from one stage to another. So, with apologies to The Beatles, if "we all want to change the world" of education, perhaps the change we need is not *evolutionary*, but *revolutionary*. What the revolution will look like remains to be seen, but I am becoming increasingly certain the revolution must occur. Ongoing continuous improvement is not working for all students or all schools. Oren Harari noted that "the electric light did not come from the continuous improvement of candles." Likewise, neither will the schools we need come about by continuously refining the current model. The time for revolutionary change in public education is now.

Not knowing what the revolution will look like or when it will occur must not stop us from doing everything in our power—individually and collectively—to push for it now. Individuals have to change before schools can change. When enough individuals change, we will have the schools our children need in today's society. There are many educators I have met over the past several years who are excited about joining the movement to change education in revolutionary ways. As we move forward, however, we must remind ourselves that not everyone is as excited about this type of change as we are, so it is up to us to make them excited about it, too. One way we can do this is by ensuring that any changes we make are implemented thoughtfully, following the CHANGE model for success. When change initiatives fail, people are less likely to enlist when the next change movement is initiated, instead adopting an all-too-common "this, too, shall pass" mindset. Our mission is too important and we must not fail; we must CHANGE: **Clarify** the vision for a better future. **Help** others to see the vision and support them along the way. Take time to plan, but then **Act**, boldly and confidently. Be prepared for the inevitable obstacles along the way, determining how you will **Navigate** these. **Generate** momentum and support by celebrating success and enlisting the support of early adopters. **Evaluate** results along the way, using these to ensure that change endures.

We cannot change our world overnight, but we can change our thinking, which can lead to changes in our actions. Eventually, we can change the thoughts and actions of those around us and, working together over time, we can even change our profession—and our world—for the better. Educators are ordinary people who do extraordinary things on a daily basis. Extraordinary change is hard, but no match for extraordinary educators willing to do whatever it takes to ensure that school works—for every student in every classroom.

## References

Collins, J. (2001). *Good to Great: Why Some Companies Make the Leap . . . and Others Don't*. London: Random House.

In: Sheninger, E. C., & Murray, T. C. (2017). *Learning Transformed: 8 Keys to Designing Tomorrows Schools, Today*. Alexandria, VA: ASCD. p. 23

Wagner, T., Kegan, R., Lahey, L. L., Lemons, R. W., Garnier, J., Helsing, D., . . . Ark, T. V. (2006). *Change Leadership: A Practical Guide to Transforming Our Schools*. San Francisco: Jossey-Bass.

# 2

# Changing the Way We Think About Learning

## Tony Sinanis

This chapter is dedicated to George, a true hero who took his life way too early.

## What Does Learning Look Like in Schools?

Take a minute and reflect on the notion of learning and specifically what learning looks like in school—any school: elementary school, high school or even college. Invariably, the memories evoked in our minds probably share many common features . . . probably a board of some sorts (chalkboard, whiteboard or SMARTBoard depending on your age); a teacher leading the learning, and likely standing at the front of the room; and finally, a group of students sitting back, usually at uncomfortable desks, possibly situated in rows, and receiving the information. Does that ring a bell? Sound or look familiar? I don't know about you but that is what learning looked like when I went to school. I was the receiver of information. I was not a thinker or a questioner or even an active participant; no, instead, I was charged with receiving and memorizing the information my teacher shared with the expectation that I would be able to document (aka regurgitate) it for some sort of assignment, test or essay. That was what learning looked like for me over 30 years ago as a student; it is what learning looked like for my students when I started out as a teacher 20 years ago . . . and in many places, it is what learning still looks like today for the students and educators in our schools.

Unfortunately, learning doesn't often look much different for the adults in our schools either. Think about the most recent professional development opportunity, workshop or conference you attended and consider the features of said experience. Are you closing your eyes and picturing that last workshop you attended? My guess is that it didn't look much different from the classroom setting described above—one person leading the learning from the front of the room and everyone in the audience (the adult learners in this case) sitting back and passively receiving the information. In many circles this has affectionately (not) come to be known as a "sit and get" experience because the participants are literally sitting back and getting information that they may or may not use after the learning event. While sitting back and getting information isn't always a bad thing (I can recall observing a few great lectures and keynotes), the fact is that I was a passive participant in all those instances . . . I was literally sitting and getting. In fact, more often than not, professional development happens to educators without much input from them or much clarity about the relevance of the learning or the plan for what becomes actionable after the professional development. Based on my experiences as an educator, the teachers who attend professional learning opportunities are either told to attend because it aligns with a new initiative in their school or they are asked to attend because no one else wants to go and the registration fees were already paid. Again, we see learning experiences—not that we can say with any certainty that learning actually occurred—that are passive, static and disconnected.

## What Is Learning?

Defining learning is like asking someone to define the concept of love—it is a somewhat abstract notion that we have all experienced, we can all probably talk about the feelings associated with it and we might be able to describe what it looks like, but actually defining it is an entirely different story. Fortunately, there have been dozens of psychologists, sociologists and researchers over time who have taken on the task of defining learning. While there are many variations of the definition, here are a couple of examples that capture the essence of learning as it is defined in most spaces:

> Learning has been defined functionally as changes in behavior that result from experience or mechanistically as changes in the organism that result from experience.
> De Houwer, Barnes-Holmes, Moors, 2013

> Learning is about any experience for a person that leads to permanent capacity change and not necessarily biological in nature or related to age.
> Illeris, 2017

The common threads are immediately visible—learning is about a change in behaviors; learning is about experiences and subsequent changes; and learning does not happen in a silo or as a result of someone's biological makeup. Learning is a process or journey that a person embarks on that then impacts their thinking, actions or opinions moving forward. Learning is about a permanent change in a person. Learning is about being informed and doing things differently because of what was learned. Learning is about social interactions. Learning is about thinking and then thinking differently. Learning is about living and changing over time.

Learning is not a straightforward process that simply revolves around information provided by others. Learning is not passive or easy. In fact, learning is a lot of work—a lot of hard work that can push educators to a point of discomfort. Alison Eyring, CEO of Organisational Solutions, recently developed a powerful analogy between learning and an oyster when she said, "The challenge of learning by experience is like sand in the oyster; it's irritating and uncomfortable at the time, but you can end up with a beautiful pearl." (Smart Brief, 2017) What an amazing analogy—learning isn't mindless or uncomplicated or momentary; instead learning is a time-consuming journey that will likely be irritating and uncomfortable, both literally and figuratively, because the end result will be change. Whether a change in behavior or a change in thinking, learning will lead to change and change can be unsettling and difficult for people. But learning can also yield beautiful results, much like when the pearl emerges from the oyster, because learning can provide people with opportunities that, while inconceivable at the start of the journey, are pregnant with possibility. Learning, when allowed to unfold in a meaningful way, can help people change, evolve and develop into a better version of themselves.

Eyring went on to connect the notions of learning and development because ultimately learning is about someone's ability to develop and grow. The research about development speaks to the fact that 70% of people's development comes when they have certain experiences that present a challenge, like reviving a failing project/student/lesson; implementing new procedures, structures or processes; handling a challenging parent/educator; or stepping into a more comprehensive role. What about the remaining 30%? Well, 20% of development is support provided by educational leaders or colleagues, and the last 10% of development is actually formal, structured learning. This is it—this is what learning looks like in life. Learning is development and it is a lot of work that requires the learner to be actively engaged and have ownership over experience. Learning can be annoying, beautiful, messy, without answers and life changing all at the same time if we create the conditions to let our students and educators actually learn.

## How Can We Redefine Learning in Our Schools?
## By Being Lifelong Learners

The current definition and manifestation of learning in our schools (passive information consumption, one person leading the learning and mindless regurgitation) needs a reboot and reframing because we know too much about learning to neglect the information and not evolve our practices. I would argue that in many cases the actual process of reflecting on what learning looks like and unpacking the big idea begins and ends with the development of the school district mission or vision statement. Take a moment, jump on the internet and search for different school district visions or mission statements and see what you find. Invariably there will be at least one statement about learning and often that statement will read something like this: "In Happy Town School District we are dedicated to nurturing and fostering lifelong learners and critical thinkers." The irony of that type of statement is the unlikelihood that the educators in Happy Town School District actually defined what learning looks like in their district and how that will support the development of lifelong learners in their classrooms. This is why we need to hit the reset button and start over. YES—it is time to reset because learning needs a better definition and our learners need access to more meaningful learning opportunities. Let's start by learning about learning in schools and redefining the experience for our educators and students.

Before addressing how we can change the way we think about learning in our schools, I am going to jump ahead and consider what type of learner our schools should be developing and supporting during the typical academic experience. Think about your typical student who walks into your district at about 5 years of age to impatiently start kindergarten and then, in an instant, that same learner is walking across the stage at age 18 during high school graduation eagerly awaiting the start of college. What do we want for that student? What skills should that student possess? How do we want that student to define himself or herself as a learner? While the possibilities are endless, I strongly believe that our goal should be to nurture lifelong learners by building on the competencies and sociocultural experiences our students have before even entering our schools.

We can no longer view our students as empty vessels that need to be filled with information because passive learning is not learning. Passive learning, which is what we still see in many classrooms across the country, is temporarily retaining information for the purposes of successfully completing a summative assessment and then forgetting most of it. Is that what we want for our incoming kindergartener or that high school graduate? I don't think anyone would answer YES! Instead, we should be giving our students access to learning opportunities that will add to their skill set and build their competencies so they come to see themselves as lifelong learners.

With that in mind, I want to consider what constitutes a lifelong learner and how we can promote and support that mind-set in our schools. I am making this jump because I think it is important that we plan backwards when it comes to changing the way we think about learning in our schools. We need to start by defining what a lifelong learner looks like so we can determine what learning behaviors should be exhibited in our schools to support the lifelong learner and then construct the foundation where our beliefs about learning will be rooted. While a lifelong learner can be defined differently depending on the setting (*I encourage you to work with your team to finalize a list that works best for your community based on what you want for that 18-year-old high school graduate*), I do appreciate the following characteristics from Christopher Knapper (2006) because they are heavily rooted in the concept of learning, which is the anchor for this chapter:

◆ People plan and monitor their own learning;
◆ Learners engage in self-evaluation and reflection;
◆ Assessment focuses on feedback for change and improvement;
◆ Learning is active, not passive;
◆ Learning occurs in both formal and informal settings;
◆ People learn with and from peers;
◆ Learners can locate and evaluate information from a wide range of sources;
◆ Learners integrate ideas from different fields;
◆ People use different learning strategies as needed and appropriate;
◆ Learning tackles real-world problems;
◆ Learning stresses process as well as content.

Check out that list. Isn't that what we want for our kids? Don't we want to encourage active self-directed thinkers who learn with and from peers to reflect on the different ways to tackle real-world problems? Think about the definition of change—it is about experiences with others that permanently change us. Learning is about ending up at a different destination that leaves you changed and potentially changes the conditions in your surroundings. In fact, every educator should print out this list of the characteristics of a lifelong learner and make two copies to serve as a checklist—one for themselves and one for each child in their classroom or school. The checklist for the students could be shared so each child can self-monitor while the teacher is also keeping track of what experiences the child has had, and needs to have, on their journey towards being a lifelong learner. The other copy of the checklist is for the teacher, who should also be embodying the qualities of a lifelong learner. The checklist for the educator will be critical because it will ensure that the educator will see themselves as a learner first and teacher second. It will also help to hold the educator accountable for their own growth, evolution and development. And finally, aspiring to be a lifelong learner will allow the educator to serve as an incredible model and mentor for every student. That is some powerful stuff because when a student sees their teacher as a learner first, something changes in that learning community. It is no longer the teacher's classroom; instead, it is a shared space where inquiry, problem solving and collaboration are the norms; it becomes a space where learning happens and everyone can feel it.

Now that we have generated a list of characteristics for what it means to be a lifelong learner, we need to unpack how learning needs to change. When thinking about the possible evolution of learning in our schools, for both students and educators, there are two areas that need to be addressed—the thinking about learning and the actual learning. The thinking about learning starts with a shared definition, an understanding of what learning is and what structures are necessary to promote learning. The thinking about learning is rooted in what educators believe philosophically based on their understandings. On the other hand, the actual learning speaks to the practices that unfold in our districts, schools and classrooms that promote and support individual and collective learning experiences. The actual learning is about the behaviors educators exhibit after they have established the non-negotiables to help promote meaningful and sustainable learning. In the end, the process of thinking about learning and the actual physical manifestation of learning in our schools requires lots of learning, the development of ideas and changes in practice.

## Step 1: Thinking About Learning

Let's begin with the norms we need to establish in order to change the way we think about learning in schools. Consider the following principles for what needs to be in place when thinking about how we define learning in schools:

- ◆ Learning is self-directed because it is inspired by what matters to the individual;
- ◆ Learning is primarily a social construct by collaborating with others and learning through social interactions;
- ◆ Learning is about supporting sustainable and permanent change.

I would argue that if everyone keeps these three principles at the core of how learning is defined within their school or district, then they will begin to make the necessary shifts to change the way learning happens in schools. To help begin and support this work in your school or district, I would like to offer context for each principle so a common understanding is at the foundation of the work.

### Thinking About Learning Principle #1: Learning Is Self-Directed Because It Is Inspired by What Matters to the Individual

In order to maximize the learning experiences for our children, we must arouse and maintain their interest because they will then actively participate in their learning. This is where the idea of personalizing a child's education comes into play. We must move beyond merely differentiating instruction (i.e., harder work for the smarter children and easier work for the needier children) and look for ways to personalize instruction. If a child exhibits certain strengths, interests or significant background knowledge in any given area, then we must ensure that our schools tap into these strengths and interests to help the child learn in the most meaningful ways possible. Again, the focus must shift from how we teach to how we make sure that our children learn. The rich and meaningful learning experiences that our children will carry with them for years, which will ensure that they are educated individuals and will shape their lives' trajectories, will likely come as a result of the "how" and not the "what."

This notion of "how" begins with understanding that sustainable learning experiences, for both students and educators, must be self-directed on some level. Self-directed and passion-based learning allow for ownership and an increased likelihood of transfer to other contexts and situations so that behaviors change moving forward. This is especially true for our educators. Let's revisit professional development for moment. Typically professional development opportunities are either ones that educators are directed to attend or they select based on a specific topic that might be relevant to their context (Guskey, 2000). While we know that educators need continuous professional development opportunities to support their efforts to sustain positive learning communities within their schools (Sorenson, 2005), we must change the direction in which professional development typically flows. In other words, professional development no longer has to originate from beyond or above the individual (e.g., being directed to attend a workshop by a supervisor). In a digital age of socially connected networks, in which information is continuously available, a reimagined notion of development should include the self-directed dimension that allows the individual to personalize their learning to help meet the needs of the organization. By empowering the individual to take responsibility for their learning, which often comes as a result of interactions with members of a personal learning network, we can help educators shift the narrative about development as an externally oriented occurrence (something that happens to them) and redirect the "responsibility" for development toward the individual. Remember, learning is about change and specifically a change in behaviors; so if we can change our approach to learning, we can ultimately change learning.

## Thinking About Learning Principle #2: Learning Is Primarily a Social Construct So Collaborating With Others and Learning Through Social Interactions

Social learning theory refers to personal experiences within a specific context and social aptitude (Wenger, 2000). Wenger argues that within a social learning system, which could apply to any context, learning is defined both socially and historically. Any knowledge developed is a result of displaying competencies defined in social communities, which in the case of this study would be the school or district (or beyond if we recognize that digital platforms can remove all physical barriers). We need to understand that every social interaction within, and beyond, our schools leads to learning because social interactions are external experiences that impact, inform or shape our behaviors.

With a basic understanding of social learning theory, we need to ensure that our students and educators have opportunities to collaborate, share and learn from each other. That means that our learning spaces, both our student classrooms and the spaces we use to facilitate learning for our educators, must be comfortable, flexible and allow for meaningful exchanges. Desks that are lined up in rows will not allow for this type of work; a heavy reliance on "independent work" will not encourage collaboration or social learning; and public behavior systems where students are penalized for talking will make collaboration, the noisy and messy kind, the exception, not the norm. We need to allow our learning spaces to be noisy and buzzing with exchanges, questions and discussions because these are the experiences that will lead to learning and, in the end, potentially change behaviors and practice.

The same goes for the educators in our spaces, whom we should encourage to collaborate and learn beyond the context of our physical environments. We are limiting our educators if we are just asking them to interact with grade level colleagues or only other educators within the building or district. There is a wealth of information beyond our schools, so let's not limit our educators to each other. The idea of educators developing a PLN, network of peers, or mentors, with whom they can learn, work and grow, speaks to a professional development model that could be accessed more often as it is built on the pillars of social learning, which we know to be an effective way to learn. Gerard, Bowyer and Linn (2007) suggest that educators prefer professional development activities that engage them in work with other educators, which again reinforces the concept of educators being growing professionally in a collaborative fashion built on the all-important social construct that is learning.

### Thinking About Learning Principle #3: Learning Is About Supporting Sustainable and Permanent Change

At the core, learning is about change; it is not about keeping things the same and retaining information for a short amount of time. Learning is about altering the way we think, changing the way we behave and reconsidering the way we live. We must remember this principle because this is the most important one if we are actually going to change the way we view learning in schools. There is nothing temporary about learning because if there is meaningful learning happening, there will be development and change.

Let's think about the students who enter our schools without the ability to read or write. After a certain amount of time, and being exposed to a variety of strategies and skills, most children will learn to read and write and because of these newfound abilities our students will be changed forever. In fact, barring a significant medical crisis, our students will never unlearn how to read or write and their lives will be permanently changed because now they can locate and evaluate information from a variety of sources. Because of the ability to read and write, our students will be able to think in a different way and critically consume information that will make learning, and the subsequent changes, a new norm.

When thinking about permanent change for educators, consider the evolution of how grades are recorded and shared with students. When I went to elementary school, grades were handwritten on a paper report card that was given out three times a year to families and was returned the following day after it had been reviewed and signed. Fast forward a few decades and most districts have adopted online grading systems that families can access through a digital portal. Grades are visible 24/7 and a parent can track their child's progress over the course of a whole semester instead of just seeing the grades on that paper report card. This integration of a digital resource has completely changed the way grades are recorded and shared with family and, barring some unexpected crisis, educators will never go back to the paper report card.

While I realize not every learning experience in our schools will be as transformative as learning to read and write, if we can always ask ourselves how we and our students have been permanently changed as a result of any given learning experience, then we will keep that reframed definition of learning at the core of our work. This will be critical when considering how authentic, sustainable and actionable our new version of learning is for our kids and fellow educators. Remember, learning is about a permanent change. Are you ready to commit to constantly changing and being consumed by recurring feelings of discomfort? Then you are ready to reset how you view learning in your space and begin to reimagine education.

## Step 2: The Actual Learning

In order to execute a successful educational experience in terms of actual learning, which would be personalized for each child to best meet their needs, we must successfully shift the focus from the "what" to the "how." As referenced earlier, too often the focus in our educational institutions is on what the children are learning, how much of the curriculum is being covered and what materials are being used to teach the various concepts. Although these are important points to consider because they do impact our children, they cannot become the focal point of said educational experiences and do not constitute meaningful learning experiences in isolation. As Dewey repeatedly points out in *Democracy and Education: An Introduction to the Philosophy of Education*, we must always be mindful of what we give our students to do as opposed to what we give them to learn because doing is ultimately learning. We cannot merely communicate information to our students, lecturing for example, and expect that the students have learned everything just because we talked about it or "taught" it (please remember that teaching does not always result in learning). Instead, we must employ a variety of collaborative, active and hands-on instructional approaches and techniques that raise the level of student engagement and challenge our children to construct their own knowledge and understandings based on what they are doing in the classroom. We must create conditions that allow for self-directed learning to be the new norm. We must remember that education is about constructing understandings, not just being given a lot of information. Dewey (John Dewey, n.d.) states, "They (*educators who employ methods that are successful in formal/traditional education*) give the pupils something to do, not something to learn; and the doing is of such a nature as to demand thinking, or the intentional noting of connections; learning naturally results." This statement needs to be the crux of every educational vision or mission statement if we are to ensure that all the experiences we construct in schools are true learning opportunities. Our educational institutions need to challenge our children to think because thinking is the basis for all intelligent learning and development of understandings. We must move away from this current push of standardized tests that assess low-level comprehension skills through multiple-choice questions (and we must disconnect these results from teacher evaluations, but that is a whole other chapter) and challenge our children to employ higher-level thinking skills, synthesizing and applying knowledge in different contexts and settings because that is learning.

Considering the ideas presented by Dewey over 80 years ago, let's continue the learning reset by reflecting on the practices and activities we need to integrate in order to change the way we experience learning in schools. While we framed the theory and thinking earlier, the time has come to unpack the practical side of learning. To that end I offer the following principles for what learning could look like in schools:

◆ Learning is about recognizing that the process and problem solving are more important than the product;

- ◆ Learning is about communicating understandings in ways that matter to us;
- ◆ Learning includes some choice while working towards a common goal/vision.

I would assert that if all educators keep these three principles in mind when planning what learning looks like within their school or district, then they will successfully make the necessary shifts to change the features and practices around learning. To help begin and support this work in your school or district, I would like to offer suggestions for each principle as a way to frame what the actual learning could look like when students are actively engaged.

### Actualizing the Learning Principle #1: Learning Is About Recognizing That the Process and Problem Solving Are More Important Than the Product

More often than not, the emphasis during any given learning experience within schools is the end product. What are students going to produce at the conclusion of this lesson or that unit to communicate their learning? The product, and specifically the way it looks, becomes such the focal point that educators miss opportunities that present themselves during the learning journey. And let's be clear, the product isn't driven by the students (we will unpack that in the next principle) but instead every detail is planned by the educator. It's like embarking on a project-based learning journey and leading all the learners toward the same end product and not allowing yourself, or the students, to get immersed in the inquiry, which is where the learning happens. So, how do we make that shift happen so that the focus is on the process and inquiry? Here is an example:

- ◆ Instead of having students fill in worksheets or write in response to the same prompt, make a shift to the workshop model in your writing instruction so that students explore different genres while trying out various strategies and skills that are modeled by the educator during a mini-lesson, small group or 1:1 conference. That way, for example, when students have finished writing a personal narrative piece, the majority of the learning time wouldn't be spent on developing the perfect final draft (heavily edited by the teacher); but instead the learning happens when students experiment with the craft of writing by incorporating dialogue or descriptive language or powerful leads. The work in this model is in the development of skills, strategies and competencies; not necessarily mastering any one of them but being exposed to them and successfully incorporating them to lift the writing and support the writer's evolution. In the writing workshop model, the learning happens when we teach the writer, not the writing, because the writer develops the skills and learning is about development (By the way, this can easily be tweaked for the educators in your space by not necessarily only holding them accountable for meeting a goal but also challenging the reflect on the journey towards meeting that goal).

### Actualizing the Learning Principle #2: Learning Is About Communicating Understandings in Ways That Matter to Us

After embracing principle #1 and reconciling the fact that learning happens during the inquiry phase, which means the emphasis should consistently be on the process and not the product, you can now shift the focus to the assessment of learning. We know that assessment can look different depending on the educator or learning space but I think we could all agree that every learning experience should have some assessment component. Now, what the assessment looks like and how it engages students is another topic altogether, but in the end, the main driver behind the development of the assessment is typically the educator. In my experience—and I was totally guilty of this as a classroom teacher—our students have little choice in how they are assessed and how they communicate their understandings. The time has come to change that because communicating understandings is an opportunity for a learner to show how they have developed and what they learned so they need to have ownership over that aspect of the journey. The learning and development belong to the individual and so should some part of the assessment. To that end, let's stop using just the standard test or one-size-fits-all culminating project and instead let's give our learners some choices in how they exhibit their understandings. Here is an example:

◆ Instead of having every child engage in the same research project, where the teacher assigns the focus, and the end result is the same book report, try incorporating a form of genius hour and have your students drive the learning. Ultimately genius hour is about students doing research around a topic they are passionate about or interested in so they can learn as much as possible and communicate the learning in a way that matters to them. We have all seen the animal research project where each child is assigned a specific animal by their teacher and then each child produces the same diorama at the end. Don't get me wrong—I love animals and dioramas can be awesome, but where is the emphasis on the learning in that situation? In the traditional form, it is teacher directed and product driven. With a slight tweak, students can decide which animal they want to research and the focus of the research can be centered around solving a problem, such as considering how animals will adapt as a result of climate change, and in the end, they can present their research in a way that matters to them. One student might create a PSA video that they post to YouTube and share through social media while another student might create a multimedia newsletter using a cloud-based platform so they can reach a broader audience. In the end, every student will successfully communicate their learning but they will have a choice to do it in a way that matters to them. Remember, learning is about self and the ability to critically consume and produce information and understandings (*By the way, this idea can easily be tweaked by having educators reflect on their goals for the year in a way that matters to them—not everyone has to fill out the same form*).

**Actualizing the Learning Principle #3: Learning Is About Some Choice While Working Towards a Common Goal/Vision**

By embracing and integrating the first two principles, you will successfully begin to make the shift from traditional learning experiences, which often don't involve much learning, to a more collaborative and learner-driven environment where choice and voice become part of the new norm. By supporting choice, we are encouraging self-directed learning and empowering the learners to consider the whole journey and create learning priorities. This is a key component to ensuring that the individual owns the learning—giving them choice to dive into learning experiences that matter to them and support their priorities while helping them develop and grow. One word of caution though: be mindful of anchoring the learning in some collective goals and a shared vision because we don't want everyone running out there and learning about a bunch of random stuff because that could splinter and fragment the organization and ultimately the learning. Here is an example of what this might look like:

◆ Try incorporating an EdCamp-style learning opportunity for your educators that is anchored in a current theme, instructional focal point or initiative (ugh, the dreaded new initiative). What is an EdCamp you ask? It is the "unconference" without formal workshops or presentations; it is a group of educators coming together to discuss and unpack specifics topic or ideas. The point of #EdCamp, in my humble and limited opinion, is an important one—it is an opportunity to take control of our professional and personal development and dive deeper into the ideas and topics that interest us and support our passion for all things education. #EdCamp is ours—those of us who embrace self-directed learning opportunities control the #EdCamp experience. The point of #EdCamp is to be in a space with other passionate educators who are in the business of enhancing their skills in the hopes of impacting students and the entire learning community in a positive way. So, if you are ready to try an EdCamp, but don't want it to be all over the place, you could create a themed EdCamp of sorts that is anchored in a shared goal or vision. For example, if your school is focused on social emotional literacy, all the sessions at your building EdCamp might be centered around SEL but everyone will still have a choice in what they learn based on their own priorities. Remember, learning is a social construct that should be self-directed and an EdCamp can be a powerful way to accomplish that goal (*By the way, this idea can easily be tweaked for a student-led EdCamp*).

## Are You Ready to Change the Way You Think About Learning?

There you have it—the call to action for changing the way we look at learning in our schools. Are you ready to make the change? Please make sure you're ready because this is challenging but important work; this work is critical to the sustainability of education in our country, which is constructed on the notion of learning. This goes beyond reform, and even deeper than a transformation; this is about going back to a basic physiological understanding of learning and using it to reimagine how we learn in schools. The time has come to go beyond the multiple-choice test or five-paragraph essay and encourage real learning. We need the kind of learning that leads to development and permanent change as a result of meaningful collaborative experiences and the integration of new knowledge. Remember learning is not passive or easy. In fact, learning is a lot of work—a lot of hard work that pushes educators to a point of discomfort. Learning, when allowed to unfold in a meaningful way, can help people change, evolve, and develop into a better version of self. Learning is the key on our journey to creating a world of beautiful pearls!

## References

Sorenson, R. (2005). Helping new principals succeed. *American School Board Journal*, 192(4), 61–63.

Guskey, T. R. (2000). *Evaluating Professional Development*. Thousand Oaks, CA: Corwin Press.

De Houwer, J., Barnes-Holmes, D., & Moors, A. (2013). *Psychonomic Bulletin & Review*, 20(4), 631–642.

Illeris, K. (2017). How We Learn: Learning and Non-Learning in School and Beyond. London: Routledge.

http://www.ciea.ch/documents/s06_ref_knapper_e.pdf

http://wenger-trayner.com/wp-content/uploads/2012/01/09-10-27-CoPs-and-systems-v2.01.pdf

Gerard L. F., Bowyer J. B., & Linn, M. C. (2007). Principal leadership for technology-enhanced science. *Journal of Science Education and Technology*, 17, 1–18.

http://www.johndeweyphilosophy.com/books/democracy_and_education/Thinking_in_Education.html

https://www.yumpu.com/en/document/view/53938218/giving-effective-feedback-w-fred-miser-md-the-r-scope

Clark, R. (2003). *The Essential 55: An Award-Winning Educator's Rules for Discovering the Successful Student in Every Child*. New York: Hyperion.

http://www.ciea.ch/documents/s06_ref_knapper_e.pdf

https://www.ted.com/talks/rita_pierson_every_kid_needs_a_champion

# 3

# Changing the Way We Think About Relationships

## Kayla Delzer

This chapter is dedicated to the thousands of young people in the U.S. who attempt suicide daily. You are loved!

When I was preparing to give my first TEDx Talk, "Reimagining Classrooms: Teachers as Learners and Students as Leaders," back in July 2015, I knew exactly how I wanted to begin and end the talk. Just like in writing, how you begin is important because it hooks the reader, and how you end the piece is crucial because it is what the reader will likely remember most. In my mind, the greatest successes I have seen in my classroom and the schools I have worked in all have one centralized focus: foundational positive relationships. The beautiful thing about being in a relationship is that there are other people involved, and it is not just all about you.

When I opened my talk, I spoke about a little boy in my second grade class who approached me on the first day of school telling me that he hated school and that I might as well send him home right then and there because this was going to be, and I quote, "my worst year ever." He yelled at me that he hated school and he hated teachers. I remember getting down to his 7-year-old level, smiling at him, and responding calmly by telling him that this year was going to be different than his other years in school. I promised him that he was going to love school this year.

Our first day together was a rough one to say the least. On the last day of the second grade school year, he had to be paged over the loud speaker multiple times because his mom had been waiting for him and she was growing impatient. You know what was holding up that little boy down the hall in our second grade classroom? He was refusing to let go of our last hug. He was crying uncontrollably. He had a fabulous year in second grade, and he loved school. It will not be the STEM lessons or the genius hour projects he worked on that he will likely remember. Rather, he will remember that his second grade teacher hugged him at the door. He will remember the love notes I wrote to him and the lunch dates we shared. He will remember how valued he felt as a human being, and not just as a student or, even worse, a test score. I reassured him that this was not the end of our relationship, and that he would be hearing from me often. This was not goodbye, but only toodles for now.

Hundreds of thousands of views later, the message of powerful relationships still resonates. In fact the most quoted line of the entire talk is this: "Relationships between students and passionate teachers will always be the foundation of successful classrooms."

## Relationships Between Educators and Their Students

I once had a principal approach me a few weeks into school saying he noticed how much effort I was putting into teaching our class expectations, routines, and norms. In his next sentence, he expressed concern that I had not dove deeply enough into our content yet. He asked me when I was going to get going on all the curriculum. I told him that the first six weeks of school were foundational for the relationships I needed to establish and nurture. How could I expect students to learn from me if they did not understand me or trust me? I convinced my principal that I had a handle on everything and that I knew exactly what I was trying to do. As a result of this investment up front, we did not spend much time later that year dealing with management or expectations. Sure, some students needed reminders from time to time, but for the most part we could focus on learning and growing together. My students averaged a growth of 1.9 grade levels that year academically according to our end-of-the-year standardized test (on which, by the way, relationships are not measured). I am confident that we would not have seen as much growth if we had not taken the time early in the year to put the focus where it needed to be: relationships and growing as a classroom family. The following ideas have been classroom tested and are approved by fabulous educators around the world to help empower your students and strengthen your relationship with them:

- ◆ **Establish a new tradition to deliver words of affirmation consistently.** Each Friday, I write love notes to every single student in my class and I stick them right to their mailboxes. I do not write the same message for every child, nor do I write paragraphs for each child. Each child receives a simple sticky note with a unique comment or note from me about something I appreciated or noticed that week. Oftentimes, my students collect these notes in their take-home binders or inside of their lockers. They take such pride in receiving an individualized love note. And you know what's even cooler? Seeing my kids begin to write love notes to each other and even me. I started to collect the notes throughout the year and displayed them around my bookshelf. I wanted to show kids that I valued their love as much as they valued mine. I have really grown in that respect throughout my career. During the early years of my teaching, if a student told me they loved me, I would often reply with a "thanks" or an awkward hug. I was trained not to be my students' friend and not to get too personal or close with them. I even had an educator once tell me not to smile until December! That does not work for me. My mom, Deb Hoerth, is my inspiration in all things elementary education. She was my kindergarten teacher, and now in her forty-second year of teaching, she epitomizes what it means to love kids, and I do not recall a single day that she did not smile at us. As a third grade teacher, I tell my students I love them often even if they do not say it first, and #lovenoteFriday is a favorite tradition of mine and the students I serve. Regardless of whether you serve ten kids or hundreds of kids, if you make this tradition or something similar an intentional priority, it will become a reality in your school.

◆ **Attend your students' activities outside of school.** I cannot even begin to count the number of hockey games, baseball games, gymnastics meets, basketball practices at the YMCA (yes, you read that right), swim meets, dance recitals, or Lego league events I have attended over the past ten years. At the beginning of each quarter, I text families asking for the schedule of extracurricular events their children participate in. I explain that I think it is imperative that students know I value them as people and that all of their interests matter to me. Most of the time, parents are surprised that I would take time out of my non-contracted personal life to support their students. For me, I cannot imagine it any other way. Obviously, I cannot attend every event of every child, but I do make every effort to attend at least one event of each child. Yes, I am spending a couple of hours on a weeknight or a Saturday at the event, but the look on the child's face when they glance over to the sidelines and see me is invaluable. Also, the two-hour investment I make on a Saturday pays huge dividends for the entire school year. A modification of this idea comes from Katie Van Dam in Coolidge, Arizona. She puts up a large calendar in her classroom where her students write their special activities like baseball or soccer games. She is able to see which events she can attend, and she said her students use the calendar to attend each other's activities as well. That's a win-win!

◆ **Set up summer reunions for your class.** I know everyone's summer schedules can fill up fast and things can get crazy quickly, but keeping up with your students after the school year is over is imperative. Students need to know that you care about them long after the school year is over. The start of summer does not need to also signal the end of a relationship. Veteran educators: think about how many weddings, baptisms, and graduations you have attended over the years. You made a lifelong impact on those students, and you meant enough to them to have been included in their very personal life events. This summer, I attended a baseball game where over two-thirds of my former students were playing. I received a text message from a mother of a former student asking if I could attend the game. I was in town that week and I said I would be honored to come! She put the word out to the other parents and they decided it would be fun for me to surprise the kids. You should have heard the screams and seen the excitement when I walked up to the field. I felt like Jon Bon Jovi or something! We also have a whole-class reunion planned to meet up at a Redhawks base-ball game. Other ideas I have used in the past include popsicles at the park and meeting at a movie theater. You can keep it simple and do what works best for you. The important thing is maintaining contact with those kids when the school year is over.

◆ **Start each day off with a positive tone!** Every morning, my students line up outside our door to enter our class-room. Students have their take-home binder out and ready for me to check, and they also are ready with a secret handshake, hug, or high-five for me. I greet the students by name and complete our individualized morning rit-ual. I ask how they are doing, and they ask how I am. I often wonder how many kids just got off a loud or crazy bus, or had a hectic morning at home. I think about how many kids just want me to see them, really see them, and acknowledge their existence. It is easy, quick, and effective. It gives me a barometer for how each child is feeling com-ing into that school day, and it sets the tone for learning.

◆ **Have lunch dates with your students**. If you are any-thing like me, I try to maximize every second of the day, including my lunchtime. I can usually be found scarfing down a salad in my classroom while answering parent emails and prepping for an upcoming lesson all at the same time. Call it a working lunch, I guess. I try not to do this every day. Once, twice, or sometimes three times a week, I have lunch dates with my students. Students earn these dates with me by getting student shout-outs for exemplary effort or attitude. If multiple students earn dates and all students agree to it, we have lunch bunches and everyone brings their lunch up to our classroom to eat. I have found I can really connect and learn a lot about my kids over a quick lunch break. And my students are more likely to open up to me about their feelings about home, what they are reading or writing about, what is working or not working for them at school, their friends and more. The pressure is down and it feels very informal and safe. An iteration of this idea comes from Sarah Glover of North Smithfield, Rhode Island. She holds a "coffee talk" each morning where she meets with one student for ten minutes to talk about anything the student wants. She drinks her coffee, and the student has a choice of milk or juice. I am tossing around the idea of possibly subbing out morning work or wake-up work altogether for Coffee Talk with one student per day.

◆ **Create a leadership gallery**. In our classroom, you will not see a traditional seasonal bulletin board that gets swapped out throughout the year. Instead, you will see framed eight-by-ten photographs of each of my students with different leadership traits printed right on the picture for all to see. This display serves as a simple reminder that we are a family, and that we strive to be the best leaders we can be every day. I try to make our classroom feel less like a classroom and more like a home. This little touch is just one of the many ways I strive to do this.

There are hundreds of other ideas that could work in your classroom or school. Please do whatever fits your flavor and fulfills your needs. You know what works best for you and your students.

## Relationships Between Students

On Tuesdays, educators from nearby states come to observe in my classroom. The day has been informally named "Observation Tuesday" by my students, and they look forward to having visitors come to our classroom. In fact, they often ask where the visitors are coming from and what to expect. When I was doing a post-observation chat with some visitors on one particular Tuesday, the teachers and principal said it was so refreshing to see kids treating each other like family, and that it must be so nice as a teacher to have a class that does not need to "deal with behaviors all the time." The comment really struck me oddly, and in the long run, I ended up taking it as a compliment. Of course every classroom has its struggles and things to work through. We work through all sorts of behaviors, ideas, beliefs, and problems daily. The beauty of putting relationships first in everything we do is that respect is appreciated and valued and not just expected. "Dealing with behaviors" takes up a lot less of our collective time and we are able to focus on other things, like learning! What follows are a few practical suggestions about establishing and sustaining the relationships your students have with each other:

◆ **Have a morning meeting**. In our classroom, right after our morning routines, we hold a morning meeting. The four components of our morning meeting are: greeting, share time, game time, and reading the message. The message is something I write on the board with news, classroom happenings, upcoming learning, and a question to answer each day. We use the model established by Responsive Classroom. I have found over the years that it is absolutely critical to give students time to talk and share about what is going on in their lives. Morning meeting is a perfect place to be open, safe, and comfortable. Additionally, in my experience, if students are not given this time to talk at morning meeting, they find the time throughout the day to talk about what's on their mind, and sometimes that time is right in the middle of my reading mini-lesson or whole group instruction. Morning meeting is the perfect time to share and connect with other kids who are going through similar things, and it is a time for us all to get to know and trust each other more. Morning meeting also allows me to nurture the relationships I work so hard to establish at the start of the school year. Our morning meetings at the beginning of the year can last up to thirty minutes. As the year goes on, the meetings are anywhere between ten and fifteen minutes. Those are minutes I would not give up for anything.

◆   A twist on this idea comes from Samantha Neitzke, a teacher in West Fargo, North Dakota. She likes to hold an end-of-the-day meeting where students take the time to recognize the awesome things they observed in each other throughout the day. She has found it really helps to build strong connections between her kids. Another teacher in West Fargo, Kaia Hassel, uses a closing greatness circle at the end of every day for the last five to eight minutes where students take the time to share positive actions that they saw in each person and the character quality that they possessed in that action. This strategy is based on the Nurtured Heart Approach. For example, a student might say, "Tori, today I saw you help out Chris when he was struggling with this math problem. That shows that you are a compassionate leader." Modeling this explicit language and the structure of this circle has created an environment of support and encouragement.

◆   **Give immediate and meaningful feedback**. Jen Jones, Reading Specialist at Hello Literacy in Raleigh, North Carolina, uses an idea she coined "Praise Phrases" with students. Students wear a lanyard with 100 meaningful, positive phrases attached for easy accessibility. These phrases are a simple yet effective way to give immediate positive verbal feedback to one another. The generation of students coming through our doors each day demand and deserve immediate feedback in multiple forms. As connected learners, they thrive on it. Praise phrases replace overused ones like "Good job!" with fresh, creative ones like "Kaysen, your brain is smokin' hot." In addition, Praise Phrases are deposits in my students' emotional bank account and feed the soul for daily positive affirmations and immediate feedback that so many students (and adults) are hungry for. Furthermore, I implemented something called Feedback Friday in my classroom this past school year. Each Friday, my students would log in to our Seesaw digital portfolios to review each other's work and leave meaningful feedback that praised, questioned, or gave suggestions for ways to improve.

◆ According to W. Fred Miser (Fred Miser, n.d.), author of *Giving Effective Feedback*:

Feedback is an objective description of a student's performance intended to guide future performance. Unlike evaluation, which judges performance, feedback is the process of helping our students assess their performance, identify areas where they are right on target and provide them tips on what they can do in the future to improve in areas that need correcting.

◆ Peer-to-peer feedback is a large part of what we do in our classroom to help us all improve, grow, and learn from failure.

◆ **Implement *The Essential 55*.** *The Essential 55* skills were developed by Ron Clark of Atlanta, Georgia. According to Clark (Clark, 2003):

Creating the type of environment where everyone supports each other and shows appreciation for the thoughts and abilities of others makes a world of difference in a classroom or in any other group of people who are trying to work together.

◆ Each week, one of our objectives is the *Essential 55* skill of the week. Some weeks, we implement and practice two skills. Skills range from holding the door open for the person behind you to answering a question with the question in the answer. Growing up, my father, Ken Hoerth, placed an extremely high value on manners. In fact, I remember vividly as a junior in high school a time he dragged me back into the office to tell the secretary "thank you" for my absence excuse note. I want to ensure my students have that same high standard, and implementing *The Essential 55* amped up the respect, accountability, and citizenship in my classroom tremendously.

The overarching message here is that students will learn more, love school, and create lifelong friendships in classrooms and schools where these approaches are the norm. There are many more programs and ideas that are not listed here. Again, find what works for you to create a safe and nurturing environment where students engage in relationships even greater than friendship, where they become part of a family. After all, schools should be places kids run into at the beginning of the day because they are so excited to be there, rather than places where kids run out at the end of the day, excited to leave.

## Relationships Between Educators and Families

I love teaching. I mean, I really love my job and just about everything that it entails. In the spirit of being transparent with you, I have to admit I struggled in my early years of teaching with writing the weekly newsletter to communicate what was happening in our classrooms. I found that it was taking up hours of my Thursday nights. So, I pushed the weekly newsletter to Mondays, and then I found I was giving up my Sundays to write the thing. I began to loathe Sundays, which used to be one of my favorite days of the week. I knew most parents read the newsletter and appreciated knowing what was happening in our classroom, but I found it hard to compose each week. As the digital world continued to evolve, I convinced myself that there must be a better way to let parents know what was happening or upcoming in our classroom. In January of 2012, I decided to start my blog, *Top Dog Teaching*, as a way to communicate with parents and share pictures of things that were happening in my classroom. Parents became engaged immediately, and we had over 1,000 page views in the first week. Since then, the blog has become just one way I reach out to families and nurture relationships with them. Here are other practical suggestions to try out right away:

- ◆ **Create video newsletters**. In addition to our classroom blog, I began outsourcing the weekly newsletter to my students. At the end of the month, students brainstorm things we have learned in addition to exciting or note-worthy upcoming events. Students pair up to create short video snippets, and we splice all those clips into one video that becomes our video newsletter. I post it on our blog and share the link with parents. Everything that would normally go into the newsletter I used to type is now being shared by students who are owning their learning and leading in our classroom. It has been a beautiful transition that was originally inspired by co-author Tony Sinanis at his school in New York.

- ◆ **Make a phone call home to each family by the end of the first quarter**. I make it a point to have my first individual contact home to a parent be a positive one. I have a calendar in my planbook, and I mark off the families I call right in the book. The point of the first phone call is for me to share something I am loving about their child at school. I do not just say that their child is awesome. I name something specific that I noticed and valued. Authentic feedback is key. I also have students call home to share exciting news with their families for events both big and small. Parents and guardians seem excited and joyful when receiving this call, and it really makes an impact down the road on my relationships with families. Parents are much more likely to problem solve with me later in the year if they already trust me and have a positive relationship established. Plus, what parent or guardian does not like hearing how awesome their child is? Melanie Lloyd, teacher in Newcastle, NSW, Australia, suggests having a list of parent names at her desk for the first few weeks of school. This helps her greet parents with any type of communication to build the relationship from the very beginning.

◆ **Connect families using the Seesaw app.** As I mentioned earlier, my students are adding different artifacts of their learning to their digital portfolios each day and giving one another priceless feedback. Another aspect of the Seesaw app that I really value is the ability to connect parents to their child's journal. As soon as my students post something to their journal and I approve it, a notification gets sent to that child's parent or guardian that there is activity in their child's Seesaw portfolio. Parents or guardians then have the ability to comment on the work or like the work. Multiple families expressed gratitude for having that peek into their child's thinking and work throughout the day. I love that families are engaged and that kids are getting even more feedback on their work.

◆ **Connect families through social media.** In our classroom, families can choose to connect with us on three social media platforms: Twitter, Instagram, and Snapchat. Students in my class complete a digital citizenship curriculum I developed, and upon receiving a passing score, students earn the right to take over the roles of Tweeter of the Day, Instagrammer of the Day, and Snapchatter of the Day. These social media accounts are essentially owned by my students day to day but moderated by me. Of course I want to be the digital role model for my students and expose them to these platforms and their power firsthand. The added bonus is that families connect with our accounts as well to get a glimpse into our classroom and everything that happens from day to day. I should also note that I spend one evening in the fall with parents and guardians where I invite them into our classroom and have my students teach them about social media etiquette, how to interact on social media with our classroom accounts, and how to set up accounts. I have a student create the schedules for all the accounts at the beginning of the month, and families look forward to seeing what their child will be sharing on social media. Parents tweet to their child, like posts on Instagram, and reply on Snapchat. While I have not dabbled with a classroom Facebook page, I know several educators who have found success with closed groups. Educators set up events that remind parents of field trips, tests, and other large events. I often get asked by educators which platform to get started with, and I do not have a perfect answer for that. I think it is important to try different approaches, because different families are on many different platforms.

◆ **Text parents about classroom happenings**. In addition to our blog, video newsletters, and social media accounts, I also use a text-messaging app called Remind to send text messages to families. I have found that not all parents utilize the digital resources I use for communication, but almost everyone can receive a text message. You can even text to landlines now and it will read the message. If a family does not have the means to provide a phone, a program like Lifeline might be able to assist. I like to schedule texts ahead of time to remind families about school and classroom events. But my absolute favorite way to use this app is to take photos of what we are doing in the classroom and ask parents to ask their child about certain and specific things we did in school that day. Gone are the days of my students being able to go home and answer the question of what they did in school with a "nothing" response. Families seem thankful to be able to fill in the blanks of what happened at school, and I am grateful that the learning continues once students are back home.

◆ **Invite parents into the classroom often**. I want parents to feel like they can contribute to our classroom and the overall experience as well as enjoy the physical space with us as much as possible. At the beginning of the year, I invite parents to sign up to volunteer by the day, week, or month. I have had many parents come in to help publish stories, sort books, or lead a math station. They also enjoy coming to our classroom for events like parties,

Author's Teas, and Pumpkin Day to name a few. Invite families to share your space often and openly.

- **Establish a Mystery Reader program**. One of my favorite ways to involve families and nurture growing readers is to invite parents, guardians, and siblings into the classroom to read a picture book to us. At the beginning of the year, I have parents voluntarily and secretly sign up for a date to come in to read one or two short books to us. They also send me five clues about themselves that I reveal to my students one at a time. All week long, we are guessing about who the reader is going to be. It is a great way to amp up the excitement for reading and include families at the same time. At the conclusion of the read aloud, I take a picture of the Mystery Reader and post it on our Wall of Fame display.

- **Hold student-led parent–teacher conferences**. Twice a year, my school district holds parent–teacher conferences. With the permission of my principal, I have been able to have student-led conferences. Students sit on one side of the table and the families and I sit on the other. My students share goals, celebrations, data, and more during the fast-paced fifteen- or twenty-minute meeting. The overall feel of the conference is more relaxed, and parents are beaming when they see their child in such a leadership role. An added bonus is that students are empowered and able to fully implement our *Essential 55* skills like eye contact, follow-up questions, and etiquette. I know traditional parent–teacher conferences can be stressful for everyone involved, so this is one way I alleviate some of that pressure. Everyone leaves the conference excited, smiling, and comfortable.

- **Hold intake conferences before school starts**. Briana Miller of Mankato, Minnesota, has two days of intake conferences with students and their families before the official first day of school. The goal is to have the students and families do most of the sharing while the teacher has an opportunity to ask questions and learn. After families have shared everything they would like to share about their child, teachers give a brief overview of what to expect during the upcoming school year.

In my experience and as illustrated above, positive relationships make or break successful classrooms and schools. They are the true difference maker when it comes to schools with happy and engaged staff members, parents, and, most importantly, students. The days of expecting kids to sit in rows compliantly and quietly need to be something of the distant past. Additionally, parents crave more contact than just a weekly newsletter or a parent–teacher conference. They want to feel connected and informed each and every day. When I work with districts or speak at conferences, I often talk about classroom learning spaces and flexible seating or education technology integration. Even then, I am always sure to mention that no matter what your classroom looks like or even if you have the best technology in the world, it will not matter if you do not put your focus and energy on people. Relationships first, everything else second. If educators believe their main focus is solely to deliver curriculum, they will quickly find out their students are performing at a much lower level than that which we as educators strive for. We are not hired as teachers to simply prepare students for the next grade level. As Rita Pierson (Rita Pierson, n.d.) said in her popular TED Talk, "Every Kid Needs a Champion," "Kids don't learn from people they don't like." This is why I always believe that relationships between students and passionate teachers will always be the foundation of successful classrooms.

## References

Moeller, A. K., Theiler, J. M., & Wu, C. (2012). *Goal Setting and Student Achievement: A Longitudinal Study.* Faculty Publications: Department of Teaching, Learning and Teacher Education, p.159.

Fullan, M. (2013). Change: Making it happen in your school and system. *Motion Leadership.ca.* Retrieved from https://michaelfullan.ca/wp-content/uploads/2016/06/00_13_Short-Handout.compressed.pdf

# 4

# Changing the Way We Think About Assessment

## Starr Sackstein

*This chapter is dedicated to the students who have thought about suicide but were brave enough to cry for help while there was still time to change the course. Life is worth it. You matter.*

What does it mean to be an "A" student? What does it mean to fail? Who gets to decide what these labels are and who should have them? As a young teacher, I shamefully reveled in my percentage of failures, indiscriminately tossing around Fs like they were air for everyone to breathe, never considering the impact or meaning of this label that I'd affixed to the children who had entrusted me with their learning. Sadly they were used to people failing them and that was what I did. I failed to provide them with meaningful learning experiences that allowed them to explore what mattered to them. I judged them needlessly. I decided wrongly.

As a matter of fact, those Fs didn't even represent learning; they represented compliance, or rather, a lack thereof. "A" students were the ones who came to class and turned work in and "F" students were their opposite. Of course, years later, I understand that these things don't show learning and often dilute the necessary communication about it. Compliance measures such as extra credit, daily homework and excessive busywork don't actually support the acquisition of skills and content toward a level of mastery; instead, it systematically kills the curiosity that makes learning fun and engaging. And that's why our most curious learners are often not our highest achievers.

"Peter is so smart, but it's all wasted potential." I often heard this regarding one of my most promising students. He was complicated, not disinterested. He'd show up to class but wouldn't comply with expectations that were put forth. Doing the teacher's proscribed work was definitely not on his agenda, but he is a voracious reader, a formidable debater and empathic collaborator, able to recognize nuance in a way the traditionally grades-motivated student is too near-sighted to see. He has opinions about things, deep things, and reasons why he feels deeply about them, not because someone told him to, but because he explored them already.

I saw what many of Peter's other teachers saw, but instead of badgering or shaming him for not doing what I wanted, I asked him why. Peter's backstory was different than I was expecting. He had deep family challenges that were more pressing and the values they had were different than mine. But he knew things and he was interested deeply in psychology as this would facilitate a deeper understanding of his own world. Instead of asking him to continue working on the same class work, we devised a plan together that would allow him to pursue his interests while practicing the same skills we were learning. He agreed to come to class during his lunch because working at home was an impossibility and we continued to get to know each other. The conversations that ensued about literature, philosophy and life were inspired, thoughtful and engaging. Peter was unique and it wasn't that he didn't like school, it was that he didn't feel that school defined him.

Simply put, he just didn't care about the label. Instead, he concerns himself with matters of interest and is generally more self-directed. And like other non-compliant students, the story helped me understand his needs as a learner and we were able to better assess his skills together through a series of dialogues and reflections coupled with the portfolio he developed. No single test would do the trick as no one situation could adequately show what he knows. After all, we need to ask ourselves, what's more important: assessing compliance measures or learning?

"A" students are often ones who play the game best, rejoicing in the label that sets them above their peers. Always focused on the task at hand, they aren't able to see the areas worth learning. And it isn't just them. School systems and communities have traditionally celebrated the highest achievers for their tenacity and wisdom. In 2017, a young man gave his valedictory address shedding light on this common misconception. Despite the fact that he had the highest GPA he acknowledged that he was not the "best" in the class. He spoke openly about different kinds of knowing that can't be quantified with weights and labels. This is the conversation we need to have when we change the way we think about assessment.

When approaching assessment, we need to consider the whole child, in a label-free manner that gives each student the voice s/he has to contribute in a meaningful way. The more we involve students in the assessment process, the more meaningful the learning and growth will be. After all, who is more qualified to tell us what they know and can do than the students themselves, especially if we give them the tools and vocabulary to do it?

Each student is motivated by something innate, and as educators it's our job to figure out what that is. Giving students a chance to unpack standards and set goals based on their individual needs and motivations is half the battle. Since learning is a highly personalized experience, the way we assess it must be as well.

Once students are able to set their goals inside of our learning context, we are better able to provide learning experiences and feedback to suit their individual needs and engage them more deeply in the learning process.

Teaching students to reflect on their learning along the way helps them grow as thinkers, allowing them to become more involved in their own process, and then when we provide them with tools to help peer assess, they become more adept at self-assessment against standards as we move each child toward mastery.

Since learning doesn't end with a letter or number in adult life, we must start to push kids toward a mindset that reflects the reality of lifelong learning. In this way we are better able to help them pursue long-term goals and grow as people and learners, and this mentality will breed future successes and grit in the face of potential failures.

## Teaching Students to Set Goals

The first part of changing the way we think about assessment is by changing who dictates what the objectives are. Since teachers and schools are currently responsible for determining what skills and content must be learned by the end of each year, we must encourage students to first understand where they are against those standards when they come to us and then set appropriate goals along the way to achieve the necessary growth. Then they can be a part of setting their personal objectives within the construct of what is deemed necessary to move forward in their learning (Since we're functioning inside of broken systemic constructs, we must do it this way. However, if we could make even bigger changes, it may make sense to have students involved even in core curriculum development).

In each of our learning spaces, students must become intimately acquainted with the standards in a way they understand. They should read them, rewrite them and then the language they use should be posted around our shared learning spaces. We must connect kids to these standards in more than just words, in our actions and in the movements of what we expect, always drawing direct parallels. Their words around standards can be referenced in conversations about learning as well as feedback being provided. The more we use student language in expectations and feedback, the better they see the results and understand the value of their own voice. As educators we must value their voices in how we assess their learning because it is about them and their own expectations about their learning.

Students can then spend time in class setting specific goals based on different tasks at hand. We can help them set meaningful actionable goals by giving them sentence starters that help them see the depth of what goals can looks like. For example, "I will improve my introductory paragraph by adding more applicable context and adapting my thesis statement to clearly help organize my essay." Students can then fill out this goal with specific strategies discussed in class during appropriate mini-lessons provided by the teacher in either small or large group instruction.

According to "Goal Setting and Student Achievement: A Longitudinal Study" in the *Modern Language Journal* in 2012 (Moeller et al., 2012), "studies have shown that appropriate goal setting, along with timely and specific feedback, can lead to higher achievement, better performance, a high level of self-efficacy, and self-regulation." And since this is the case, we must make time to teach students to set goals in our classes.

Educators of all ages can find ways to help students first unpack the content and skills needed to be successful in a particular unit. If we work to be more project-based, students can participate in project design as well and then determine what specifically they will work on based on their understanding of what the project is supposed to be showing about their learning and where they are specifically in the process.

Once students have identified a small but manageable amount of actionable goals, teachers can provide the best strategies for achieving those goals either by working with students independently or in small groups. Additionally, throughout the process, teachers should stop the whole class where applicable to address challenges that arise universally.

Goals should be cyclic in nature. Much like learning an important lesson, we often need to revisit what we've learned when it comes up again in another context. Students need to be able to go beyond mere identification of these skills and move toward the ability to self-select the tools that will help them be successful with different tasks at hand in every aspect of their lives. Setting actionable goals helps to organize the way we tackle problems every day, perhaps just not in such a formalized manner. The more we help students bring this practice into their everyday routines, the better equipped they will be to move forward in their lives once school has ended and probably help them manage the many challenges and burdens that will undoubtedly arise.

It is also important to keep goals visible so that we can hold each other personally accountable for the goals we set. Once students determine what they are working on, consider having a bulletin board where students can display what they are working on and then allow them to chunk those goals with others in the class working on the same things. This can also facilitate students reaching out to different peers not just because they are friends, but because they are working on the same skills. This kind of peer-empowered culture will help students seek each other out before going to the teacher. This space can also be used for celebration when goals are met and reflections are shared.

## Promoting Student Engagement With the Learning

Once students commit to their goals, it's time for us to give them opportunities to work toward successfully achieving them. Students should understand from the outset that failure is a part of learning, not a deterrent from it, and the more we push ourselves through "failed" attempts, the more resilient and adept we become at what we are seeking to achieve. No masterpiece was created without mistakes and the real learning happens in the exploration of what didn't work the first time. Schools have to do a better job of rebranding failure to embrace the growth mindset.

Project-based learning in lieu of traditional testing is a more accurate and transferable experience to real life. As we consider how we think about assessment, we need to realize that watching learning is an on-going experience. This solidifies why giving a grade at any given time offers a false understanding of what kids know and can do. A snapshot only lasts so long, and so as each child evolves, so do his/her level of mastery in any particular area. We need to focus less on the snapshots and more on the collage the snapshots are showing. It's the big picture of mastery that we are working toward.

To parallel life outside of school, we must offer students multiple opportunities to try to meet and/or exceed the skills required for the goals they set for themselves. As educators, we must watch, direct and provide feedback that helps them achieve those goals in a meaningful way. There are many ways to do this, but we must consider our learners when we choose. Rather than have one way, like a test, for students to show what they know, we must offer them choice and provide them time to first conceive of and then revise what they have done to really cultivate a deeper understanding.

Project-based learning offers students a chance to both practice in groups or independently the skills we want them to learn as they tackle new content together. Then after problem solving together, students should be encouraged to use the same skills on an independent project where they can apply the new learning on their own in a new way. Real mastery is achieved only after consistently working through a new skill and content and then being able to apply it without someone telling you which tool to use. It's the real ability to know what you know and use it when the situation calls for it.

Some examples of great project-based learning can also encompass different learning modalities which would allow students to showcase new learning in the way that works best for them. For example, over the course of studying one novel, rather than just have students read chapters so we can discuss them around themes that the teacher and/ or other academic determined were essential to teach, we should allow students to explore literature like they do life. What inspires them? How does it connect to their context? Instead of traditional essays, students should be able to share the depth of their understanding in a variety of ways, first in small groups to dig deeper and then in a large group and then independently.

While reading Jane Austen's *Pride and Prejudice*, students could do character studies, explore historical connections, participate in thematic tableau installments, make movies, create social media accounts, participate in Twitter chats as their characters, socialize in historically appropriate tea parties and socials and/ or write about their learning and understanding. The richness of the discussions while preparing projects are far deeper than four students participating in a class discussion while the rest of the class check their phones or languish in boredom.

Other successful projects include multimedia assignments that explore human interaction around nature, self-selected by students. Satirical movies and manifestos about topics they care about. Creating and participating in an online media outlet creating real news to share with their peers about what matters to them. True collaborative environments where they are brainstorming ideas, deciding on which ones to move forward on, developing them and revising together after providing feedback.

But it's not just in the Humanities classroom where this is possible. Consider how mathematical practices apply to the world or how the process of solving problems can be transformed into a product for kids to build. This can work with experiments in science too when we allow students to use inquiry to drive their projects in all subjects at all ages. Curiosity goes a long way and this is an easy place to add choice and voice into the how and what students are studying in our spaces, which will give us a better view of what we know about their skills and content acquisition and development.

Doing the project isn't the only way to learn, though. Students can share expertise in areas once their projects are done. Using class time to do gallery walks or screenings offers another entryway for kids to learn from each other. Then they can fold their learning from each other into what they might try differently next time. Teachers can use this time to really get kids exploring what they learned from their classmates and how it applies to their own learning.

Space in class should be delineated for this kind of work. Time is given to what we value and when students see that we value reviewing each other's learning, they will take the experience more seriously. We need for them to know that what they do matters not just to the teacher but to every learner in the space who will be seeing their work. Teachers can consider using a social media space to share their wonderings about what they learn and provide feedback through a digital formative tool so that teachers aren't the only ones providing students thoughts about their work. Feedback can be transformational and it must be allowed to be a part of the learning process.

## Teaching Students to Reflect

As students begin to move through their learning process, they should explicitly be taught to reflect. It isn't just about what they enjoyed or didn't like, but more importantly, what did they learn and how do they know they have learned it? When addressing specific objectives of the learning, they should use examples from their own work to support how they are meeting standards. It's important to help them here too.

Ask them to think about what the assignment was asking them to do. They should rephrase this in a way that makes sense to them. What skills were they asked to show? Once they have shared what they feel the assignment was asking, they should consider what they learned from it. Students should ask themselves, "What can I do now that I couldn't do before or what can I do better or what do I know now that wasn't a part of my understanding earlier?" Depending on their age, they can answer these questions directly or can write a more developed reflection that addresses them appropriately.

This is the time for students to think about their initial goals as well. Did they meet the goals they set for themselves? How do they know? Where in the work do they address the goals and how do they know it was effective? We can't let kids say it was effective because a teacher told them it was . . . we need to push them beyond that. They need to speak to how they were able to write a thesis that provided an outline for the organization of an essay or context that drew readers in. Perhaps they speak to finding the right evidence to support what they hypothesized. Whatever they suggest, they should be able to find evidence to support their assessment of learning in their own work.

Additionally, students should be challenged to think about the process of HOW they achieved the learning. What steps did they take to be successful? Where did they falter? How would they do it differently next time? In this area, we can teach students to use formative feedback they have received throughout the process to talk about approaches they have employed and why they haven't worked and if they don't know, that is okay too, as it will undoubtedly inform educators about how to instruct them moving forward.

The more we talk about mistakes or early failings, the more it becomes a part of the normal learning process. All learners must understand that getting things wrong is a part of learning how to get things right. Whether it is learning the quadratic equation and applying it appropriately, writing an essay, playing the piano or dribbling a basketball, it all takes practice and it is likely the first attempt was not perfect. Perfect simply doesn't exist, not in learning and not in life.

Students should also use this forum to discuss how older learning is connected with the new learning. What did they do before that helped support what they are doing now and how do they know?

As teachers read these reflections, prior to new learning opportunities, there is a whole host of information that can be used to help with future instruction. Teachers can use effective grouping strategies and also develop a series of mini-lessons that address areas of need based on students' understanding; teachers can then norm as well as provide more directed and individualized feedback for learning to increase on-going growth and development around a skill or content area.

## Teaching Students to Self-Assess

Self-assessment is different than reflection in that it also seeks to determine a level of mastery. We want students to be able to look at their own work as well as their peers' work in a meaningful way based on exemplars and we want them to talk about how they feel they measure up to mastery.

Teachers alone should not be making this determination. A conversation of what success criteria looks like should be co-created with students whether in the form of a rubric or a checklist, or some other alternative form. Students should be a part of discussing what demonstrates mastery and should be asked to defend their ideas. Teachers should collect and collaborate with students to ensure a consensus can be reached.

Introducing these ideas to students can start as easily as starting a unit with the intended project first. Review and revise the assignment sheet together and then determine what skills and content need to be shown to demonstrate mastery. Also flesh out the different ways students can do that. As students start to break apart assignments into pieces they can help backward plan the lessons they will need to learn in order to be successful with the assignment. Students should do this in pairs first and then independently and, lastly, discuss in a whole group. This is another opportunity for teachers to gather data for necessary mini-lessons to ensure success on the project and the enriching of the learning.

Once success criteria have been agreed upon, examples should also be selected. They shouldn't be from prior students who have completed the same project, but something similar that demonstrates the content and/or skills. We never want to give students the exact version of what mastery looks like in the exact project they are working on as that sometimes can rob students of the opportunity for creativity. They think they are being original, but they are often using the same suggested ideas. We must seek to demonstrate the necessary skills and/or content in a different way so that they are still free to come up with something original of their own.

Much in the same way, teachers need to be careful when providing feedback in the early stages, both written or in conversation. Initial ideas about moving students forward should always be started by asking students what they are working on and what they need help with. Allowing this to be a discussion led by the learning is more appropriate than the teacher dictating what is right or wrong. We should really be trying to ask questions to understand where the student is coming from so we can help direct rather than lead the progress.

These conversations should be directly related to and connected with the agreed upon success criteria, so that students are going through a self-assessment process both as they go and also at the end. Reflection supports the depth in which students will be able to share their personal evaluations.

Demonstrations of how to self-assess should be modeled regularly for students and they should practice doing it in smaller settings.

## Providing Actionable Feedback

When a student submits a reflection with all of the work s/he completes, teachers have a map for how to review it. Those reflections should address the specific goals set at the outset of the project and how the students feel about their progress on those goals; then the teacher can provide very targeted feedback specifically around the students' goals.

Rather than review student work strictly through the lens of the teacher, based on objectives decided in a solitary situation, we should see student work through student eyes using their reflections as a jumping off point. If I know a student is working on using text evidence to support their understanding of a document-based essay, then I can provide targeted feedback, showing the student where s/he is successful at meeting that goal and why it is successful. I can then identify and provide actionable feedback for areas where the student still needs to improve.

It is not enough to just show a student where s/he is doing something well or not; we must specifically say why and if it needs improvement, we must offer a solution and/or strategy for them to employ. These strategies can then be tracked by students so when they work on the same skills moving forward or continue to revise the same project, when they return to their reflections, they can specifically address the strategies they used and how successful they were.

Students should be empowered to ask for help in ways that work for them, and learning to anticipate their own needs is another skill that these metacognitive practices will foster. The more students receive actionable feedback, the better they will be at asking for help in the future and/or providing better feedback to peers inside of the formative process. Teachers must never be seen as the sole source of knowledge in a classroom. All learners are equal and are able to share expertise in different areas. That expertise is what pushes all of us to grow in the specific areas on which we are working. This can also help with intentional pairing and future expert groups in peer feedback protocols.

Students should be encouraged throughout the process to use collaborative tools like Google docs in order to use the commenting function to help provide more specific and targeted feedback through their learning processes. Not only do programs like this track the learning and revisions being done, but they allow students to start feedback dialogues, create tasks and even provide particular examples that help to demonstrate the strategies that can help improve the learning.

## Changing the Way We Understand Communicating About Learning

Assessment is far more than an isolated, end-of-unit experience for learners "to take" to show what can be momentarily captured for the sheer purpose of ensuring a cursory understanding of content and an opportunity to put a label in a gradebook. Formative opportunities must be presented all the time with directed, actionable feedback to provide the most individualized and transparent learning. It is not enough if the educator can see the growth; the student must be in on it. S/he must be an integral part of the conversation, both in filling in the gaps of what we see and also asking for help to dig deeper.

As we seek to meet the state requirements that determine mastery of learning, we need to work through other options that are open to different student learning styles and involvement. If schools begin to implement portfolio systems where students are expected to collect their learning, select their best improved pieces, reflect on the depth of that growth and then connect the skills and content to other areas of their life and learning, students will more likely become productive members of society.

The bottom line is that learning looks different for everyone and no one way is the best or right way and how we arrive at what we know isn't so binary and therefore can't be labeled adequately. Each label we present is a temporary misrepresentation of a moment that is fleeting. Report cards fail students, families and schools because by the time that snapshot is shared, like a snapchat, it has disappeared. Comments are inauthentic and pre-written. Feedback must be personalized and narrative and it should provide an action plan and educators shouldn't be the only ones writing them.

We must stop watering down the learning experience by adding non-learning components to how we assess for learning. No more arbitrary labels based on seat time or extra credit unrelated to tasks. No more compliance worksheets that prove nothing about what a child knows and can do. No more shortcuts. All kids deserve the opportunity to learn and to show what they know and we can provide that for them by listening when they speak and giving them some latitude in how they present their learning.

Today's tools and resources offer a multitude of solutions we didn't have years ago and if we utilize all the tools we have available, the better the learning experience will be for all students and that must be our goal. Assessment shouldn't be used as a tool to shame or reward or rank or create competitive environments; it should be used as a means to better understand where kids are on the mastery continuum and then provide better instruction to ensure that the learning continues to progress.

# 5

# Changing the Way We Think About Technology in the Classroom

## Thomas C. Murray

This chapter is written in loving memory of Cody, age 10. #LoveYaMan!

"I'd love to see these units become standard equipment for all students in five to ten years," was what I shared with the local reporter for her front-page story on the use of educational technology in the classroom after she came to observe and capture a lesson on what technology integration could look like. I went on: "When you give a 10-year-old child this kind of technology, it creates a solid love for learning."

Was I referencing some robust virtual reality? No. Were we 3D printing newly designed fidget spinners? No. Were we learning through some interactive, adaptive software? No.

I was referring to Palm Pilots. Yes, really. In 2002, my second year teaching, my fourth graders each had their own device. We were *1:1 Palm Pilots*.

After the lesson was finished and the photos had filled the storage card of the reporter, I began to reflect on my lesson for the day. The lesson had also served as one of my formal observations, and I figured that doing a "technology lesson" was the exact kind of thing that would impress my principal. As I thought through the various aspects of the lesson that I had just led, I was proud. My head was high. The spelling lesson had been executed exactly as I had planned.

Every student had followed each direction given. When I'd asked a question, a myriad of hands went up. Every student seemed to have the correct answer each time I called on one of them. Every student was "engaged" for the entire lesson. I had "integrated technology" from start to finish.

As a new teacher, I thought I had nailed it. With my lesson plan followed perfectly, all students engaged, technology used throughout, I thought my post-observation conversation would essentially be my principal, a dynamic instructional leader, singing my praises throughout.

The next day came and I was excited to walk down to the principal's office to sit side by side to hear his thoughts on my lesson. Like many principals will often do, he asked, "So Tom, how do you feel the lesson went?"

With my head high, and my chest out a bit, I shared that I thought it went very well. My plans had been followed, every student had been fully engaged, and our new technology investment had been fully utilized. I'm sure from across the table, I was probably smiling from ear to ear as I anticipated his incredible feedback.

"So Tom, what were your learning objectives?" he asked.

"We wanted to use the Palm Pilots to be able to . . ." I began to respond, before being cut off.

"No, Tom. What were your **learning** objectives?"

Thinking maybe he didn't understand what I was saying, I began again.

"For this spelling lesson, I wanted to use the Palm Pilots to . . ."

My principal, with whom I had a positive relationship with, respectfully cut me off again and proceeded to say words that I'd never forget.

"Tom, you're not getting it. Stop leading with the technology. Tell me **about the learning**, not about the technology."

This moment in time, during a post-observation conversation, was a defining moment in my career. I remember it like it was yesterday. I still even remember where I was sitting.

He went on. "Tom, were all students engaged? Yes. Did every student follow every one of your directions? Yes. Did the lesson plan go exactly as you had planned? Yes."

Then he dropped it on me.

"However, you planned and executed that lesson because the technology could do something, not because it was the best way to learn something. Although every student was engaged, following your directions, and enjoying the technology, what did students **actually learn** in the process?"

Not only were his words humbling as my ego had been brought back to reality, but in retrospect, *he was spot on.* I could have chosen to allow his honesty and pushing my mindset to damage the solid relationship we had built. Let's face it. My pride was hurt. I could have put my head down and chosen never to use the technology again—especially during an observation. But, the more I thought about it, I came to the realization that he was right. I had planned my lesson around the technology that I had available, instead of focusing on the best way to learn something. I realized that from that moment on, I needed to maintain a laser focus on creating high-level, authentic learning experiences first and that the *technology was a tool—an amplifier, not the desired end goal.* Pedagogy is first; technology supports.

What I learned that day is that *technology use will never overcome poor pedagogy.* In the words of Michael Fullan (Fullan, 2013), "Pedagogy is the driver. Technology is the accelerator." As such, technology *can absolutely* accelerate and empower student learning experiences. However, it can also amplify poor instructional practices.

*The teacher and his or her instructional practices, not the technology, is always the difference maker.*

## What Does the Effective Use of Edtech Look Like?

In recent years, school budgets have remained relatively stagnant. However, on the whole, spending in educational technology has continued to climb year after year. Monitor social media and it won't be long before you see claims about how a particular device or tool is a "game changer" or how a particular tool will "revolutionize education."

It's highly evident that we need to change the way we think about technology in the classroom. With great pedagogy, technology can help open new worlds of learning. With poor pedagogy, low-level learning experiences can become the norm.

Technology will never be "the game changer" or the thing to "revolutionize education." Contrary to the beliefs and practices of some, it is not, nor will it ever be, a silver bullet. It is educators that are—*and will be*—"the game changer" every single time. Our work is first and foremost about people, not apps or devices. We cannot lose sight of that.

Having a "technology first" mindset is dangerous. Leading with technology and not learning, as my principal emphasized early on, can amplify poor teaching practices. As such, using technology for low-level tasks will ultimately yield low-level learning experiences for our students.

I believe this type of low-level technology usage is sadly the norm, not the exception. It is why, in my opinion, large-scale studies, such as the one released by the Organisation for Economic Co-operation and Development (OECD), titled *Students, Computers and Learning: Making the Connection* (2015), indicate the following (p. 3):

> Students who use computers moderately at school tend to have somewhat better learning outcomes than students who use computers rarely. But students who use computers very frequently at school do a lot worse in most learning outcomes, even after accounting for social

background and student demographics. The results also show no appreciable improvements in student achievement in reading, mathematics, or science in countries that had invested heavily in ICT [information and communication technology] for education. And perhaps the most disappointing finding of the report is that technology is of little help in bridging the skills divide between advantaged and disadvantaged students.

I believe the findings of this OECD report, and others that show similar results, parallel the types of technology use that are prevalent in many, if not most, classrooms. Low-level, drill-and-kill technology use leads to low-level learning. Every time. Compounding such instructional practices over time will undoubtedly have a negative effect on student achievement, and lead to low-level learning outcomes, as seen in global reports such as OECD.

Fifteen years after the conversation with my principal, I was working at the central office as the technology director for my school district. I was the person responsible for budgeting, purchasing, and disseminating the technology throughout the district. I was in the third year of that role, and we were continuing to expand our 1:1 device-to-student ratio efforts.

It was the final budget meeting for the upcoming school year—the one where the school board ultimately votes to pass, or not pass, the spending plan for the following year. Being in a cabinet-level position, as we worked through the budget, the funding for technology was brought up. With a vision of moving to a 1:1 device-to-studio ratio, we were looking to increase device expenditures significantly for the following year. Late that evening, as we worked through the various aspects of the proposed budget, the school board president looked to me and asked the following question:

"Tom, if we spend this additional [dollar amount] for devices next year, will student achievement increase?"

Years later, when I think back to that question by the school board president, the person ultimately responsible for signing over taxpayer money for all expenditures, I realize what a great question it was. Although we can argue over how such "student achievement" should be measured, or if it was the "right" question, what he was ultimately getting at was, if we were going to invest in all of that additional technology, would it actually make a difference for students? An excellent question indeed.

To answer such a question, and to rethink the use of technology in the classroom, we have to understand the types of practices that have *proven* effective. On the flip side, to effectively leverage technology as a tool to accelerate student learning, one should understand the types of technology-infused practices that have proven to have *little-to-no impact* on student learning.

The Alliance for Excellent Education, based in Washington, D.C., teamed up with world-renown researcher, Linda Darling-Hammond, and her team at the Stanford Center for Opportunity Policy in Education (SCOPE) in 2014 to explore that notion. *Using Technology to Support At-Risk Students' Learning* (Darling-Hammond et al., 2014), one of the most comprehensive meta-analyses on the topic, outlines what the research points to that actually works to support student learning, and ultimately, what's a waste of time and money.

The report highlights three key areas surrounding the effective use of technology (Sheninger and Murray, 2017, p. 65):

1. **Interactive learning**. The interactive use of technology can enhance student learning and, ultimately, achievement by providing multiple ways for learners to grasp traditionally difficult concepts. Interactive learning opportunities have become more robust as adaptive content and systems have evolved in recent years. In these systems, the content levels up and down based on a student's ability; in other words, it adapts to a student's level of need. When leveraged for interactive learning, students become active users—not passive consumers of content.

2. **Use of technology to explore and create**. When students are given the opportunity to leverage technology to explore and create, new learning can be accelerated. When this is the case, students are able to create and develop new content rather than absorb content passively. When

empowered to explore and create, students also demonstrate higher levels of engagement, more positive attitudes toward school, higher levels of skill development, and self-efficacy.

3. **Right blend of teachers and technology.** When students have ubiquitous access, particularly in environments with 1:1 student-to-device ratios, digital experiences can be blended into the learning environment to extrapolate concepts and maximize learning opportunities. In these environments, students can access the "right blend" of direct instruction and technology-accelerated learning. Student voice and choice play an important role while the teacher gives the needed level of direct support. Technology use is most productive when experiences combine the "structured learning of information with collaborative discussions and project-based activities that allow students to use the information to solve meaningful problems or create their own products, both individually and collectively" (Darling-Hammond et al., 2014, p. 15).

Today's devices provide incredible potential for those who use them. For a few hundred dollars, it's now possible to purchase more computing power than what put men on the moon half a century ago. However, walk down the hallway in the average school, and you'll see classrooms where technology is being used for dynamic, authentic learning experiences, and across the hall where identical technology is being used for low-level, drill-and-kill experiences. Coined "The Digital Use Divide" in the 2016 National EdTech Plan (Office of Educational Technology, 2016), the following image (Figure 5.1) depicts the contrast between low-level, consumption-based "Passive Use" and higher-level "Active Use."

Contrasting the notion between "passive" and "active" use can help educators decipher which technology-infused instructional practices can best support student learning and ultimately, are most worth the precious instructional time invested.

Another supporting resource for technology use and reflection, created by Dr. Ruben Puentedura, is known as "SAMR."

# DIGITAL USE DIVIDE

While essential, closing the digital divide alone will not transform learning.
We must also close the digital **use** divide by ensuring all students understand
how to use technology as a tool to engage in creative, productive,
life-long learning rather than simply consuming passive content.

PASSIVE USE

ACTIVE USE

**FIGURE 5.1**

*Source:* From "Section 1: Engaging and Empowering Learning Through Technology," by
the U.S. Department of Education, Office of Educational Technology, 2015. Available:
http://tech.ed.gov/netp/learning

SAMR, a model used to help educators understand various levels
of technology integration, stands for **S**ubstitution, **A**ugmenta-
tion, **M**odification, and **R**edefinition. Puentedura outlined each
area of the model as follows (Figure 5.2):

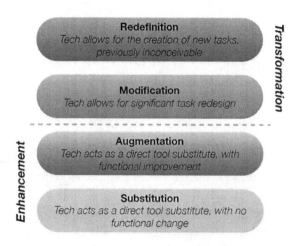

**FIGURE 5.2**

*Image credit:* Dr. Ruben Puentedura. Available: www.hippasus.com/rrpweblog

The lower half of the SAMR model ("below the line") is recognized as the "Enhancement" stage, where technology is utilized to alter, for instance, what may have been non-digital measures. An example would be moving from writing a five-paragraph essay on modern culture using pencil and paper to using a computer to type the same essay and save it digitally. The task itself hasn't changed, yet moving to the digital realm may enhance efficiency and productivity for the user. As contexts move from analog to digital, it's important to remember that it's not uncommon for innovation to begin at this level on the continuum.

Moving "above the line" to the "Transformation" stage, the fundamental nature of what's occurring has been altered due to the influence of technology. At this level, the task itself has been completely changed. Synchronously collaborating with students in another country on an essay and production project that compares and contrasts the modern culture prevalent in the two different nations, and then creating a presentation that will be shared in real time in both classrooms, would be an example of leveraging technology at a redefinition level. Simply put, without the technology, the task would not be feasible. In comparing the two experiences, moving to higher-level use would lead to deeper learning opportunities for students.

As educators move across the integration continuum, thinking through the various levels of SAMR can support a reflection on the effectiveness of technology integration for the task at hand. Principals can utilize the model to help teachers think about moving "above the line" (i.e. as seen between augmentation and modification) in their instructional design and implementation. As school leaders help teachers visualize and understand what's being asked of them, they in turn are modeling the expected classroom practices. In the same light, telling teachers they need to change, yet *not providing* the needed resources, frameworks, and supports, is an outcome of poor leadership and modeling. In these cases, change will be minimal and resistance will often be high. Such practices lead to pockets of innovation. To scale innovative work and ideas, high-octane school leadership empowering a dynamic school culture, with a foundation built on trust, are imperative.

Side-by-side comparisons of SAMR with other commonly used instructional frameworks such as Bloom's Taxonomy or Webb's Depth of Knowledge, or the contrast outlined in the "Digital Use Divide," can also support educators in planning more personal and authentic learning experiences for the students that they serve. Take a moment to compare, contrast, and reflect on the following four frameworks/models (Figure 5.3):

| Level | SAMR | Bloom's Taxonomy | Webb's Depth of Knowledge (DOK) | National EdTech Plan |
|---|---|---|---|---|
| **Highest** ^ | *Redefinition* | *Create* *Evaluate* | *Extended Reasoning (4)* | *Active Use* |
| | *Modification* | *Analyze* | *Strategic Thinking (3)* | |
| | *Augmentation* | *Apply* *Understand* | *Skills & Concepts (2)* | *Passive Use* |
| **Lowest** | *Substitution* | *Remember* | *Recall & Reproduction (1)* | |

**FIGURE 5.3**

Few would disagree that one of our main goals as educators must be to help students become independent problem solvers who can think critically, adapt to new situations, and become productive members of a global society. Thus, focusing on the needed skill attainment for tomorrow's workforce through higher-level instructional design today, becomes our moral obligation. Utilizing such models and frameworks can help teachers conceptualize a depth progression and thus further skill development, ultimately supporting their design process.

While models such as SAMR can be a support for instructional design, it is important to consider that, as with any framework or model, communication, context, and practical use are vital components to successful outcomes. For instance, it'd be easy for one to come away thinking that all technology use must be at the "Redefinition Level" or that all activities where technology is used must fall into the "Active Use" category if the frameworks are used poorly. Yet, using particular tools for efficiency purposes and at the Substitution Level is often perfectly fine. In the same light, very high levels of learning can absolutely occur *without any technology use at all*. Keeping a common sense approach with these types of supports is key. Any experienced educator will tell you that the utopian-esque idea of maintaining these levels at all times is not feasible. However, what is feasible is a conscious effort to make learning experiences high-level and authentic, as often as possible, and leveraging technology tools to amplify and accelerate the learning in meaningful ways throughout the process.

As we wrestle with the various aspects of such classroom use, we must tackle, head-on, some of the latest trends. With all that is known from the research regarding the effective use, it's important to alter the conversation from the latest tool, app, website, or trend, to a laser-like focus on instructional practice.

Today's educator conversations are often littered with commentary about how so and so "went paperless," how someone has everything digital in a particular online platform, or how they use a particular suite of software for all aspects of daily instruction. Although not inherently bad, these conversations often focus on tools and not on high levels of instructional pedagogy. Something like "going paperless" in and of itself indicates nothing about student growth and learning. A paperless environment can be highly interactive and filled with authentic learning experiences, or extremely low level, and exacerbate the ineffective digital drill and kill methodology.

When technology is leveraged to create a more teacher-centric environment, or increase the amount of time on low-level tasks, student learning opportunities suffer. To reflect, what kind of devices do you have in your school or classroom? Are the devices being utilized as a digital worksheet storage hub or a pathway to unleash student genius? (Figure 5.4)

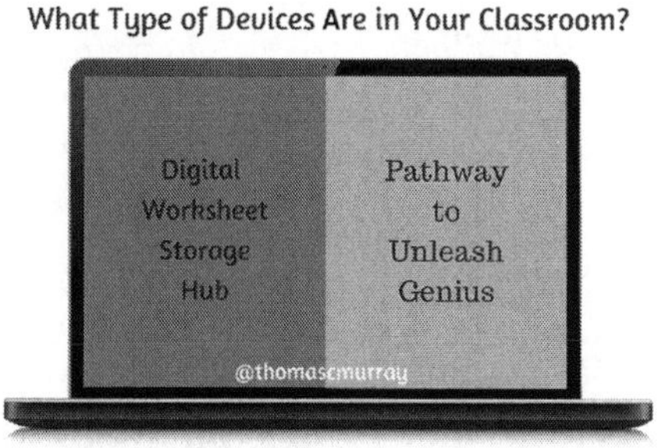

What Type of Devices Are in Your Classroom?

| Digital Worksheet Storage Hub | Pathway to Unleash Genius |

@thomascmurray

**FIGURE 5.4**

## The Latest Trend: Evaluate, Vision, and Proceed With Caution

Expanding the discourse on the effective use of edtech, let's quickly examine three current and popular trends: 3D printers, Makerspaces, and the use of STEM/coding tools, as many schools throughout the world are investing a considerable amount of money in each area.

### 3D Printers

In recent years, 3D printing has become all the rage. Like any technology tool, 3D printers can be a dynamic support in creating authentic, personal experiences, or they can be a colossal waste of money. Consider the following two scenarios:

Scenario 1

The local elementary school uses funds raised by the parent organization to purchase the building's first 3D printer, which is stored in a common area—the library. In early October, the second grade teacher, Caden, brings his class to the library to experience the new equipment. For 45 minutes, students listen to the teacher as they watch the printing of the building's mascot. At the end of the class period, the students cheer as the small duck that they watched print is removed from the printer.

Scenario 2

At a local high school, Paisley asks her students, "With the tools that we have available, including our new 3D printer, what problems can we help solve?" After some critical thinking and research by students, one student suggests that they collaboratively design 3D printed hands for kids around the world who were born without one. The students then spend time designing, testing, redesigning, and ultimately printing hands to be sent to those who need them. (This scenario is loosely based

on "The Hand Challenge," which can be found at www
.handchallenge.com.)

In Scenario 1, which in my opinion represents many student
experiences with 3D printers in schools, little to no learning
occurred. Simply watching something print should be the end
result—*the reward*—for the hard work and the learning that has
occurred throughout the design process. In Scenario 2, students
leveraged the technology to explore, create, and design, leading to an authentic learning experience (not to mention learning about aspects of culture, empathy, etc.). When using these
types of tools, the vast majority of the learning occurs during
the design and creation process. Skipping this portion of the
experience will ultimately yield low-level learning opportunities,
and quite often, be a waste of time and money.

## Makerspaces

The maker movement—a relatively recent return to constructivist
theory, initially made popular by Jean Piaget, and later by Sey-
mour Papert—pushes learners to construct their own knowledge,
through active learning opportunities. Makerspaces can take
many forms, and on the whole, the term itself can often have
various meanings. Some contain opportunities and tools that
infuse educational technologies, where others may be purposefully low tech. Consider the following scenario:

> The new Makerspace at the local elementary school con-
> sists of dozens of materials, from outdated computers,
> to molding clay, to Legos. Many of the materials have
> been donated by the community, while some have been
> purchased through the limited budget made available by
> the school's principal.

Few will argue that having a space for students to design and
create has many drawbacks and the notion falls in line with constructivist theory. However, the space itself can be highly effective and help provide personal, authentic experiences, or, when
lacking direction or vision, the same space can be minimally

effective. When dynamically implemented, Makerspaces present a problem to solve, or a design thinking process to take part in, or a theme to create around. At a minimum, a vision for the learning to occur is needed.

I believe that the most powerful Makerspaces leverage the interests of the learner. These spaces connect constructivist learning opportunities to a student's authentic interests, passions, and personal experiences. Simply making Play-Doh and Legos available for students in and of itself won't translate into dynamic experiences. Creating spaces that are ripe for exploration, creativity, innovation, and socially catalytic experiences, however, will.

## STEM/Coding Tools

Another recent edtech trend has schools investing heavily in STEM- or coding-related tools. From apps to robots, schools can spend anywhere from a few dollars to thousands of dollars on these types of tools.

Similar to 3D printers, when using coding tools it's *the process, not the product* where the most amount of learning takes place. Quite often, schools are investing in such tools only to provide low-level experiences. Buying the few hundred-dollar robot to use an app to drive it around the classroom provides no more learning than driving a remote control car in decades past. If schools are celebrating the driving of robots and seeing these as effective learning experiences, their thought processes are misguided. It's the process—the actual coding or design—where the learning takes place and, ultimately, what matters most. When designed well, these experiences *can be* highly personal and authentic for student learning. With poor instructional design, hundreds, if not thousands, of dollars can be wasted. Yet again, it's the process—*the pedagogy*—that matters most, not the tool or latest device.

Simply put, 3D printers, Makerspaces, and coding tools can *absolutely* be incredibly dynamic resources to help provide highly personal and authentic student learning experiences. Yet, it's important to recognize and understand that the exact same tools can lead to low-level learning, poor student experiences, and ultimately a waste of time and resources. What types of experiences are your students having with the tools that your school is investing in?

## Equity: A Key Aspect of Edtech in Schools

As we examine the opportunities that become available when leveraging technology tools, educators must keep the notion of *equity* at the forefront. A myriad of evidence indicates that equity in opportunity and equity in access both remain significant issues. From the types of rigorous courses that students have available, to the types of tools they are able to access, to the availability of home connectivity, there are vast gaps in opportunities for students—even for one of the richest countries in the world.

A review of data from the Pew Research Center indicates that of the 29 million households with school-aged children, approximately 5 million families, one out of every six with school-aged children, lacks access to high-quality broadband at home. Furthermore, almost one out of every three households with children ages 6–17, with incomes below $50,000, do not have a high-speed Internet connection (Horrigan, 2015). The data also indicate that Hispanic and African American families make up a disproportionate percentage of those families without access. This means that millions of children sitting in our classrooms each day lose connectivity the moment they leave their school campus.

Schools discussing possibilities related to classroom technology use must consider those without access at home. Handing students devices, and expecting them to do work that they cannot access without Wi-Fi, puts some of our most needy children in a terrible, and unethical, situation. Quite often this happens without the adults ever having any clue that the student has been put at a significant disadvantage, and in turn widens the disparity gap of those in need. How does your school handle this equity issue?

As schools work to support those in need of home access, a myriad of innovative ways to support students have come to light. In places such as Spartanburg 7 in South Carolina, school leaders collaborate with the businesses within their borders, and ask owners to consider supporting students by providing guest access on their business Wi-Fi. A variety of businesses signed up to support students, and a map of all available locations was created to show families the various locations throughout the community where they were welcome to work if they needed access outside of school. Such a collaborative effort not only builds community, but also shows those families most in need that they matter and that their needs are recognized.

One national nonprofit, EveryoneON (www.everyoneon.org), is working to eliminate this digital divide by making high-speed broadband service, computers, and free digital literacy courses accessible to those who do not have access. This organization is a tremendous support for families without access and is a tool that can be leveraged by educators from coast to coast. In many cases, families can obtain low-cost broadband for as low as $10 per month, purchase refurbished equipment for a fraction of the normal cost, or receive training in digital skills—for free. Is your school leveraging this type of dynamic resource to support those in need? If not, how are you addressing this need in the classroom or throughout your school district?

From Wi-Fi on buses, to making hotspots available for students to sign on, to collaborating with the community for public Wi-Fi, school leaders are finding ways to help families get connected and take a step forward in breaking the chains of poverty. Equity is a moral obligation, and supporting those most in need must always remain at the top of our priority list.

Advances in technology in recent decades have given today's modern learners, and those that lead them, opportunities that have never previously been feasible. With the expected exponential growth in this sector in the future, these opportunities will only continue to expand.

So, how will you remain hyper-focused *on the learning* and avoid getting caught up, as I did with the Palm Pilots, in the latest trend or fad? Most importantly, how will you provide authentic, personal experiences for students and how can technology make those experiences even more robust?

Regardless of the position that you may hold, from pre-service teacher, to entering your final year in schools, *you* have an opportunity—*every day*—to make a lifelong impact on those which you are privileged to serve. Today's technology, and that which will be created in future years, can provide the tools, access, and connections needed to further build relationships so that your impact can flourish and expand to deeper levels for generations to come. May we never forget, high tech or low tech, that the foundation of all that we do is, and always will be, grounded in loving and caring about the children that we serve, and doing whatever it takes to open their world to new, and better, possibilities.

## References

Darling-Hammond, L., Zielezinski, M., & Goldman, S. (2014). *Using Technology to Support at-Risk Students' Learning*. Stanford, CA: The Alliance for Excellent Education and Stanford Center for Opportunity Policy in Education as cited in Sheninger and Murray, 2017.

Horrigan, J. (2015). The numbers behind the broadband "homework gap". *Pew Research Center*. Retrieved from www.pewresearch.org/fact-tank/2015/04/20/the-numbers-behindthe-broadband-homework-gap

OECD. (2015). *Students, Computers and Learning: Making the Connection*. PISA, OECD Publishing. Retrieved from http://dx.doi.org/10.1787/9789264239555-en

Office of Educational Technology, U.S. Department of Education. (2016). National education technology plan. *Future Ready Learning: Reimagining the Role of Technology in Education*. Retrieved from http://tech.ed.gov/netp

Sheninger, E., & Murray, T. (2017). *Learning Transformed: 8 Keys to Designing Tomorrow's Schools Today*. Alexandria, VA: ASCD.

# 6

# Changing the Way We Think About Mental Health

## Joe Mazza

This chapter is dedicated to Amy Bleuel, founder of Project Semicolon. Amy died in 2017.

Anyone who has flown in an airplane has heard their flight attendant run through the preflight safety checks, including demonstrating what to do if the oxygen masks fall from the ceiling in the event the cabin's oxygen levels fall to a certain level.

But what if we followed these instructions when we thought about how we help students struggling with mental health issues? As adults, do we model the way for students in this area? How many conversations are we having with our colleagues about real-life challenges, and things that are rooted outside of the school setting? Are we afraid others will judge us or overlook us for opportunities based on certain stigmata? Have we come to grips with our own day-to-day challenges? Do we practice what we preach to school-aged children? Or do we pretend it doesn't exist, hoping nothing bad will ever happen to anyone we know? As I inch closer to 40 years on this Earth, I'm continuously surprised at how American society enables mental health concerns to spread—that is the silent crisis of my generation, and one that reminds me how much room we have to grow as people.

We, at least, discuss the problems with students, and work to provide support. For students, we offer social-emotional learning (SEL) curriculums, counselors, themed events and cross-curricular opportunities to break the ice on these conversations. We expect there to be challenges as students develop, and allocate resources to support them the best we can.

But what if "the best we can" isn't (and has never been) good enough? What if educators were brave enough to model the way, to open up about how they and others handle the day-to-day challenges of life? If we could model how life is inevitably messy, would students benefit from this perspective during the most important phases of their development? Let's take a look in the mirror as a nation when it comes to mental health.

## The Current State of Mental Health (Eye-Popping Stats)

One in five adults today (or 43.8 million adults) **battle** mental health challenges everyday. And most don't have it tattooed on their forehead so others can even tell, let alone respond with support. The National Center for Health Statistics recently reported the U.S. hit its highest suicide rate in 30 years, with significant increases for Native Americans, people ages 45 to 64, especially white women, as well as girls between 10 and 14. The only demographic groups that did not see a rise in suicides were black men and people over 75.

To put these statistics in perspective, let's picture a large elementary-sized school and staff.

These 2017 statistics (NAMI) translate to:

- ◆ A staff of 60 with 12 adults who struggle with mental health challenges;
- ◆ A school with 600 students equates to 120 students who already do or someday will struggle with their mental health challenges.

These are the facts the best we have them today. We can't continue hoping and praying things will change unless we make a much bigger investment in our children's well-being in *and* out of school. But in the meantime, we have to do everything we can to limit potential tragedy by taking a proactive approach at home and at school.

## Part I—Low-Tech Mirroring

If you've presenting to a group, you might have used a cord to connect your computer to a big screen so an entire room can view and/or interact. Today's technologies allow us to simply skip the cord, and mirror the content wirelessly using a process called "mirroring."

Now, taking the same premise of the teacher sharing something on their personal computer with the class, what if we looked at mirroring in a different way—through the lens of an adult committed to working *for* kids, being more open about day-to-day health and well-being challenges. In 20 years, I've seen plenty of teachers be very open and upfront about physical education, dieting and weight management—but on the topic of mental health and well-being, it is rarely exposed as a conversational topic among not only students but adults. As one of my personal mentors (whom I still haven't been fortunate to hear speak live) Brene Brown asks us, do we have the courage to be vulnerable? Can we, as educators, parents, adult role models in the lives of kids, openly discuss the shit show that is hidden behind our publicly perfect life, resume, digital footprint, etc.? Can we be real with our students, at a time

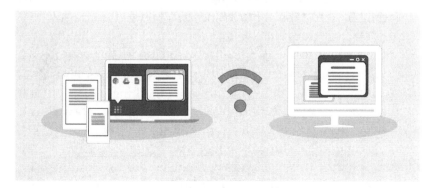

**FIGURE 6.1**

when they need to see they are not the only ones who are struggling with the day-to-day trials and tribulations of life?

---

Vulnerability is the only bridge to build connection.

---

If you believe in the Whole Child, you don't need to be convinced; we can't teach students without addressing their social-emotional needs. A once a week health class where the content is not developmentally and/or culturally appropriate doesn't count. We can do better. We must.

## Part II—On-Demand Programming the New "Current Events"?

Back in my own K–12 student days, I can recall many teachers asking me to bring in a "current events" article relating to our class discussions at various times during middle and high school. This was in the 80s and 90s, back before the World Wide Web and, of course, before social media and media marketplaces like Netflix were at our disposal.

### Netflix

Today, most kids and adults have heard of Netflix. Since its inception in 1997, the 8-billion-dollar company has grown to become a top 50 app, website and download, now drawing over 98 million users. As a parent of four (oldest is 5), I already see how, with many on-demand programming options and alternatives, my kids will have Netflix or something like it in their lives for the foreseeable future. My wife and I model (with our own ubiquitous use) Netflix for movies, do-it-yourself (DIY) resources and a few shows we like to watch during the year. For the kids, Netflix provides access to thousands of shows, movies, special segments and other age-appropriate and inappropriate options—which we as parents can customize in advance or in real time. Right now, our kids (5, 3, 1, 1) are watching little if anything that "requires" parental supervision, but as our oldest (Mark) grows up, we know the moments when we may need to intervene are right around the corner.

One Netflix show we've been watching with our oldest is called *The Hunt*, where animals in the wild are captured hunting, gathering food and prey. One of the takeaways from our viewing of this program is that predators fail many more times than they succeed. We've learned about an awful lot of sharks, cheetahs, eagles and snakes through watching their actions caught on high-definition cameras, highlighted by the narration of Sir David Attenborough, a well-known naturalist in the UK.

Full disclosure—my wife and I didn't preview the episodes and we actually thought one of the recent episodes would cause him nightmares; the one where multiple snakes take on the predator role in chase of prey, an iguana. The edited footage was really well done.

However, all it has done is further fuel his desire to learn more about them, and during our last trip to PetSmart, he asked to adopt a ball python, which has (in month three as I write this) become a daily occurrence. His pleas to mom and dad have been met by an overwhelming blend of "Are you crazy!?," "We already have a dog" and "No way, I'm afraid of those things." Honestly, at 5, Mark doesn't understand what it takes to adopt a pet and care for it, or understand what it needs to survive and thrive away from a natural habitat—all solid reasons for us to *say no* to the snake at this time.

So now the ball (python, ha!) is in our court as parents, and as educators. Should our fears about certain things (like snakes) shut down a passion and a pre-loaded context for learning within our kids? For our students?

Even though both my wife and I have always been deathly afraid of snakes, it's hard to say no to your kids when they want to learn more about something, gain a new perspective on science and biology and engage in something that gets them away from a flickering screen. Let's look at some recent data on how today's teens are spending their leisure time.

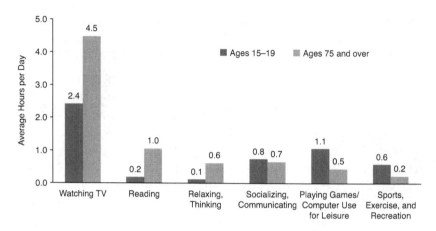

**FIGURE 6.2**

Source: Bureau of Labor Statistics, American Time Use Survey, Retrieved from https://www.bls.gov/tus/charts/leisure.htm

Studies show we're spending more time bingeing shows on Netflix than socializing with other human beings today. I share this because I believe it is the wake-up call schools and families need to start addressing the issue head-on and thinking more deeply and collaboratively, when we are tempted to warn parents to hide certain content and material from students.

So it's not even close. Today's youth are spending more time watching shows than anything else. What if we tapped into some of that content, and used (local) pop culture more as the compass for our day-to-day teaching, but especially for complicated, oftentimes delicate, content and contexts?

## The Viral Netflix Series on Teen Suicide

The hottest show on Netflix in 2017 was *13 Reasons Why*, in which a new high school student named Hannah takes her own life. Two weeks after her tragic death, a classmate named Clay finds a mysterious box on his porch. Inside the box are recordings made by Hannah—on whom Clay had a crush—in which she explains the 13 reasons why she chose to commit suicide. If Clay decides to listen to the recordings, he will find out if and how he made the list. The intricate and heart-wrenching tale is told through Clay's and Hannah's dual narratives. The Netflix production (originally a 2007 novel by Jay Asher) produced by Selena Gomez, has become the all-time #1 most watched and tweeted about series by school-aged kids.

With shows like *13 Reasons Why* being "binge-watched" across teenage demographics, mental health-related show plots are mainstream enough now that they even warrant a special Netflix rating, "RP18," which means someone under the age of 18 should view the series with the supervision of a parent or guardian. Good intentions? Sure. Realistic? Hardly. How many teenagers watch shows with their parents? This is where parents and educators have an opportunity to set the table for further dialogue in natural, non-judgmental ways. But this is not what's currently happening. We're doing everything we can to blame others, write beautifully sad form letters home to families when something bad happens and pray it doesn't get any worse. As a father of young children, I'm out to find others not willing to sit on their hands, and one day suffer the fate of a lost child like _____.

I wasn't joking about the form letters. Somehow in 2017 we still think, as educational leaders, that this one-way communication will (1) fly, and (2) help anyone feel better about the situation.

I've spoken with many school leaders across the country who "addressed" the ten-part series following with a form letter sent to parents and the community like the one used in the example below:

*May 17, 2017*

*Dear Families,*

*I am writing to inform you about a new Netflix series titled* 13 Reasons Why *and its possible impact on our students.* 13 Reasons Why *is gaining popularity and we have concerns that the series may increase thoughts of suicide among students.*

*The show is based on a novel and the story of 17-year-old girl who takes her own life. She leaves behind 13 recordings explaining the reasons why she chose to commit suicide. While the show brings up the importance of talking about suicidal thoughts, it portrays situations where youth are dealing with serious issues, from bullying to sexual assault, without getting support from adults.*

*Denver Public Schools teaches the Signs of Suicide (SOS) curriculum in sixth and ninth grade across the district. The SOS curriculum focuses on supporting students to identify warning signs of depression or thoughts of suicide and make a report to a trusted adult for support. Our school psychologist, school nurses, social workers and counselors are trained in suicide prevention and supports and, unlike some of the adults in* 13 Reasons Why, *take all reports seriously.*

*You may wish to discuss the series, or thoughts of suicide, with your child. Talk to your child about what they can do if they have a friend that is expressing thoughts about hurting themselves. As we discuss in the SOS curriculum, teach your child to acknowledge if they have a problem, be caring and tell an adult. Remind your child that there is help available if they ever feel sad or depressed. Be sure your child has the hotline numbers listed below.*

*Please consider the age and developmental stage of your child before allowing them to watch the show. We do not recommend that children with a history of suicidal thoughts, depression or mental health concerns watch* 13 Reasons Why. *If you do allow your child to watch this series, we recommend you watch it with them and discuss it afterwards.*

*If your child has warning signs of depression or suicide, don't be afraid to ask if they have thought about suicide. Raising the issue of suicide does not increase the risk. Instead, it decreases the risk by providing an opportunity for help.*

*If your child is in need of assistance, please reach out to your school mental health staff.*

*Helpful Resources:*

*Colorado Crisis and Support Line at 844–493–8255, or Text TALK to 38255*
*National Suicide Hotline at 800–273–8255*
*Safe2Tell at 877–542–7233*
*Trevor Project Hotline for Suicide Prevention for LGBTQ youth 866–488–7386*

*Talking Points for Parents: www.nasponline.org/resources-and-publications/resources/school-safety-andcrisis/preventing-youth-suicide/13-reasons-why-netflix-series-considerations-for-educators*

Since May, I've confirmed with several educators from different states that the same form letter was sent home and/or posted on school/district websites as the virality and reach of the series rose to new record heights.

In 12 years as a school principal and assistant principal, I've never found that a form letter provided a transformational approach to small or large school issues. Form letters aren't meant to solve anything, but they can buy time for the real work to be planned and orchestrated, while communicating facts to the community. They take hours to write, edit, proof, revise, approve and distribute out to the community. At the end of the day, our largest chunks of time are better spent pulling people together who want to dig deeper, and draft strategies based upon what we know about mental health, Netflix, school culture, teenagers and our current school structure. We need to leverage the human capital that exists within the organization to best meet the needs of our community. And if we've been as proactive about staff and student well-being and mental health as we have been about staff and student physical education, this team is most likely already meeting regularly, anticipating risks and opportunities and leading the change necessary through listening, empathy, innovation and empowerment. This team is already working towards promoting mental health awareness by raising the emotional capacity and self-awareness of staff and students. We know that a critical component to a mentally healthy community is high levels of self-awareness and healthy relationships.

Adults at home and at school have a responsibility to tap into what we already know is happening. *13 Reasons Why* is a widely popular show that puts mental health on the front burner and our most at-risk subgroups are likely watching every single episode. To that end why would we choose not to bring these "current events" to our classrooms, social skills groups, dinner tables and other more intimate gatherings?

We know what Netflix brings to the table. It is a means of ongoing and relatable content, and perhaps a platform parents and educators can leverage to break the ice on critical conversations vs. trying to steer kids and families away from the content "to protect them."

Change will take us out of our comfort zone, but this work is complicated and without shortcuts. Think deeper next time you go for that form letter and personalize the experience for students, staff and family members. Families and educators must "mirror" and "model" their own thoughts, ideas and early assumptions and not hold back the authentic dialogue that occurs while we process what we see in the media, and on-demand networks like Netflix. The power of family–community partnerships lies in melding the distinct areas of a child's day, and the hundreds of thoughts that the world around them prompts. This is the area where I'm not convinced we are collectively rowing in the same direction, and the consequences for ignoring youth suicide and the rise of mental health challenges like ADHD, anxiety, depression, bi-polar, and a whole list of others, is deplorable and negligent on the part of parents *and* educators. It is the not the parents' job. It is not the teachers' job. It is *our* job in working for kids.

## We Get a Redo

There will be a second season of *Thirteen Reasons Why* airing in 2018. How will this school district and others leverage the on-screen happenings in the classroom, or will it choose to send another form letter home to parents to warn them about explicit content? The content included in the first season may have caught parents and educators off guard, but will we revisit our approach with knowledge of a looming second season? Now is the time to be having these discussions locally and globally. The "current events" will be there. Where will we be if and when our number is called? Every adult with a relationship with the child needs to be empathetic, be vigilant and, most importantly, work with others regardless of his/her role.

## A Few Questions to Consider for Parents of Preteens/Teens

- ◆ Have you had a "frank" conversation with your teenager about the realities of what's in the book/movie?
- ◆ In comparison, when was the last time you took an unfiltered look at who your child is following on Facebook, Instagram, Snapchat, Twitter, etc.? The fact that you are not tech-savvy isn't a good excuse (anymore).
- ◆ How comfortable are you in handling your teen's mental health, and modeling what depression or down thoughts/ feelings look like? If you struggle, do you model getting the help you need?

## Educators—A Few Points to Consider

- ◆ Put the oxygen mask on yourself before you help the person next to you. Working in schools is not easy work. Some years are absolutely insane in terms of the pace, unexpected events, family issues, etc. Get yourself some help if you are having trouble meeting basic day-to-day tasks. Confide in a friend.
- ◆ Watch and listen via social media—What are students saying about the movie? Yes, this is the reason you need to join Snapchat.
- ◆ Curriculum aside, take advantage of the teachable moments that arise from current events heard on NPR or from YouTube clips. (We've been waiting for mental health to become a front burner topic. How will we chip away at it differently when we know it will come up?)
- ◆ Student development of ideas. As educators, we must *listen most*, with a goal to create a culture where talking about tough topics, i.e. mental health, is considered a norm.
- ◆ Staff development ideas. Read the book and/or watch the movie. Host a Voxer bookchat. Assign conversation leaders once per week for six weeks.
- ◆ Parent development. Host a powerful speaker who is a great storyteller. Screen the movie. Help start a closed Facebook group for support.

- ◆ As a leadership team, remember to document your reflections and breakthroughs, and work to make empathy-mapping part of your design process.

## For Parents and Educators

- ◆ Leadership must do what it takes to move the topic to the front burner—formal and informal leaders.
- ◆ Keep your ear to the ground. Do we have our finger on the pulse, AKA society's influence? How do you put yourself in a place to continue learning in your day to day?
- ◆ Actively network (i.e. local NAMI, #semicolonEDU, etc.).
  - ◆ SemicolonEDU Day is July 14. Educators around the world share their semicolon ; tattoos, and offer words of encouragement for others battling somewhere along the journey.
    - ◆ There is a private Facebook group aimed at supporting educators who battle mental health challenges. Two of those #semicolonEDU members have told their own powerful stories, which can be found online with a quick Google search. My post is entitled, "Let's Stop Faking It," and it's detailed below.

*https://medium.com/@Joe_Mazza/lets-stop-faking-it-5380e0aea289*

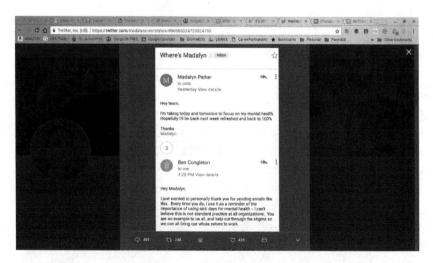

**FIGURE 6.3**

Every once in a while good news breaks that makes you feel like progress is being made in this area. The tweet shared above is just that, as Madalyn Parker screenshot her mental health day emails to and from her boss. Ben Congleton (M's boss) not only got back to her within 24 hours, but responded in a way that showed he actually cared about her. If this work is about relationships as much as we say it is, then he's nailed it, and folks would take a pay cut to work with an empathetic leader.

# 7

# Changing the Way We Think About Teacher Engagement

## Sanée Bell

This chapter is dedicated to Jadyn, "my morning greeter," age 10.

According to a 2014 report released by Gallup, about 70% of K–12 teachers reported they were not actively engaged in their work. Teachers were given a 12-item survey, which was designed to measure a range of positive workplace outcomes. Engagement was measured in three ways: engaged, actively engaged, and disengaged. Only 30% of the teachers surveyed reported that they were actively engaged in their work. Approximately 57% of the teachers surveyed reported that they were engaged, while 13% reported that they were disengaged (Gallup, 2014). Before I delve into this topic further, I want to define the types of engagement discussed in the report.

## Levels of Engagement

The engaged teacher can be described as being compliant. This teacher goes through the motions without any purpose or passion. This teacher does what is requested of him or her, not necessarily because they believe in it, but because they were told to do so. This type of teacher is on autopilot. They are not causing problems by rocking the boat, but they are not interested in making any waves either. Compliant teachers are not hot or cold, but can be considered lukewarm in their approach to their work. I believe with support or a nudge from the right influencer, this type of teacher can move up on the teacher engagement barometer.

The actively engaged teacher is committed to constantly growing professionally. This teacher owns their professional learning and sees the value in connecting with others to improve their craft. Actively engaged teachers do not view the teaching profession as work. They view their chosen profession as an ongoing passion project with endless possibilities.

In contrast, the disengaged teacher is not only unhappy with his or her work, but they want to make sure others are unhappy and unsuccessful, too. This type of teacher is a culture killer who seeks to create and spread toxic energy. They undermine any good that is occurring on a campus or in the professional lives of others. They are so miserable in their role, and probably with their life, but yet they keep hanging around instead of seeking other employment opportunities.

I am sure each of us can identify a colleague who may fall into each category. As educators, we are charged with engaging and inspiring the next generation of leaders and learners. How can we, as a profession, truly engage our students if only 30% of teachers are actively engaged in the work?

I had the privilege of hearing Brandon Busteed (2015), Executive Director of Gallup Education, share this report at a conference, and I was extremely bothered by the staggering statistics he shared. I began to reflect on my role as a leader and the responsibility in addressing this teacher engagement problem. If we believe that student engagement is the responsibility of the teacher, what role does the leader play in teacher engagement?

While the responsibility cannot totally fall on the shoulders of leaders, it is important to note that they certainly play a significant role in creating and sustaining a culture that encourages, promotes, and supports active teacher engagement. As professionals, we have the responsibility to continue to learn and grow, regardless of the working environment and leadership we may encounter, but it is my opinion that strong leadership can move the teacher engagement pendulum in the right direction. I do believe that teachers must have the desire to move from being disengaged or engaged to becoming actively engaged, but I think leaders should see themselves as part of the process in removing barriers that hinder teachers from becoming actively engaged in their work. As leaders, we have two choices:

◆ Take a hands-off approach to teacher engagement and let teachers find their own way; or
◆ Actively participate and create an environment in which all teachers are engaged.

Both approaches will yield results. A hands-off approach will lead to a small number of teachers who are engaged by happenstance, whereas an active, intentional approach will lead to a system of excellence that was purposefully designed to meet the needs of all.

## Compliance Is the Enemy of Commitment

My grandmother, who I affectionately call "Mamaw," always had a goal to complete her college degree. She began her family at a young age, and although she tried many times to complete the degree over several years, she struggled to reach the finish line. When she was in her 70s, she decided to pursue her undergraduate degree full time. She was one of the oldest students enrolled at the university. She had some challenges to overcome, but she never gave up. She connected with her purpose, which fueled her engagement level. She ultimately graduated and experienced the college life she always dreamed of, which at some points in her life seemed to be elusive.

During this process, "Mamaw" always told herself that she was going the extra mile, and then some. This saying has resonated with me as I continue to grow as a professional. Although I have always had a high level of intrinsic motivation, there have been times that I have not been actively engaged in work that I did not connect with on a personal level, and it was hard for me to go the extra mile in that situation. Teachers who are actively engaged in their work are manifestations of what it means to go the extra mile, and then some. These teachers will probably thrive in any environment regardless of the leadership they are working under; however, at some point, they could potentially burn out and move from active engagement to engagement if they are not personally and professionally connected to the purpose of their work.

How does one move from engagement to active engagement? I believe this is where identifying one's purpose becomes so critical. Simon Sinek's "How Great Leaders Inspire Action" TED talk resonated with me personally and professionally (Simon Sinek, n.d.). I used his "Why-How-What" structure to articulate my personal and professional why. This was not an easy task. I had to think introspectively about what I stood for as a person and leader. One of the most common questions asked when individuals meet for the first time is "What do you do for a living?" Most give the expected answer, "I am teacher," "I am a principal," etc., which is the response most people identify with, but how often do people state their why first before moving to the what? If we responded in this way, the answer to the "what do you do for a living?" question would sound somewhat like this:

> "I seek to inspire others to see the possible in every situation. I help others to become their best possible self by adding value to the individuals I encounter each day. I do this by building relationships with others and by using my story as a framework for understanding and empathizing with people. Being a principal is an honor and a privilege that I do not take for granted."

Knowing my why is the foundation of my engagement as a leader. This keeps me grounded as a professional and is especially helpful when I face situations that challenge my beliefs and practices. Engagement begins from the inside out.

Busteed (2015) shared that the key to being engaged is finding purpose in one's work. Although the study highlights that there needs to be a focus on increasing teacher engagement, teachers did report satisfaction with their choice to be an educator. Teachers surveyed consider their chosen profession as more of a calling than a career. I believe that most educators enter the profession with a moral purpose to inspire and "make the world a better place," but perhaps lose that motivation or passion because they don't keep their why at the center of their work. It is important for teachers to frequently revisit and articulate their why in order to maintain a level of active engagement.

In the same respects, leaders need to do the same for the schools they lead. Most schools spend a great deal of time developing a vision and mission for the school but continue to make decisions separate and apart from the vision and mission that was created. Most people within the organization probably cannot recite the mission or vision because they don't own the words on the paper, nor do they know the why behind the words that were crafted. Leaders need to engage teachers in the process of developing the "Why-How-What" for themselves and the school. Working from a purpose is a catalyst for creating an engaging work environment. When everyone knows who they are and what they stand for professionally, and as an organization, the collective group owns the work and is more likely to be engaged in the work environment.

## Creating a Community of Learners

If teachers are responsible for student engagement, who is responsible for teacher engagement? I would like to think that the same best practices that work for student learners can be applied to adult learners. The role of the leader should be similar to the teacher who taught in the one-room schoolhouse. In the one-room schoolhouse, each student was taught at their level and had the opportunity to learn from their peers.

Leaders need to be committed to identifying the individual learning needs of the teachers they are charged with leading.

How can leaders support teacher learning if they are not knowledgeable about their learning needs?

More importantly, how can leaders expect teachers to practice vulnerability if they have not established a relationship with them? Being skilled in the area of relationship building is key to moving an organization from being engaged to becoming actively engaged. Leaders who put an emphasis on relationships are skilled in meeting the individual needs of teachers. They approach each individual differently, which allows them to differentiate support and professional learning. Leaders who intentionally focus on building the culture of the organization use the collective efficacy of the group to motivate, challenge, and inspire the group.

Teachers are constantly seeking out resources, best practices, and ideas from other teachers outside of their building. As teachers become more connected through local and global networks, leaders need to leverage this desire so that teachers are also seeking resources, ideas, and support from the colleagues they see each day. By removing the barriers and walls to collaboration, leaders can create a learning community where teachers are engaging with each other organically.

Early in my career as a principal, I met with a small group of colleagues to discuss the complexities of the principalship. We also learned together by sharing best practices that resulted in high levels of learning for students. Although I was an elementary principal for five years, I had no teaching experience at the elementary level. Because of my lack of firsthand elementary teaching experience, I had a strong desire and need to learn as much as I could about effective instructional practices in the elementary setting.

These meetings were loosely structured, but they always involved observing classrooms. The principal who hosted the team shared the instructional focus areas that were currently being implemented on their campus. We were asked to give specific feedback about what we observed as it related to the campus instructional focus. Some of the best conversations occurred during this debriefing session and almost all visits resulted in us sending teachers over to observe and learn from the teachers we observed as a group. I learned a great deal from these informal collaborative sessions, and I desired to provide the same opportunity for the teachers on my campus to participate in a similar learning experience. I wanted to create a framework for teachers that would allow them to learn from each other through structured discourse and reflection about their professional practice.

Providing structure and support that allows teachers to learn from each other is an important component in creating a collaborative culture among teachers. Although the ultimate goal of any organization is for the collaboration to happen naturally, the initial structure was key to establishing the foundation for what focused, productive, collaborative learning should look like between a community of learners. I think it is important to note that before teachers feel comfortable engaging in this kind of work, a culture of trust must be established. Teachers who allow others to watch them teach are exhibiting a great deal of vulnerability. It is important to stress that the purpose of visiting each other's classrooms is not to be judgmental about one another's practice, but to learn from colleagues and gain insights and new understanding about our own professional practice. The ultimate goal is for teachers to be reflective about their own practice and to build the collective expertise and professional capital of the group.

The benefit of implementing this work on our campus was amazing. The collaborative learning that occurred across grade levels strengthened and added value to the professional core of our campus. Teachers began seeking guidance from their colleagues about how to address instructional issues, and they engaged in dialogue about professional best practices. They also felt validated about their current progress as a teacher, and they often shared with me that they were highly engaged in their work as professionals.

While teachers may have learned from each other indirectly through planning lessons and sharing resources, it is unlikely that the rich dialogue and reflection that took place at the end of the classroom visits would have naturally occurred if teachers had not been given the opportunity to observe and learn from each other. Creating a structure that empowered teachers to learn and share with each other positively contributed to the collaborative culture of learning at our school.

## Teacher Voice

One of the main aspects of the Gallup study that I found alarming was the lack of teacher voice in the profession. Teachers ranked last in comparison to other professions when it comes to saying their opinions at work matter. Teachers also reported that their supervisors had not created an open environment for dialogue, which made them feel that their voice was not heard.

Historically, our profession is one that follows the bureaucratic model. Typically, initiatives are mandated and passed down from the federal and state government to the local agency, from the local agency to the principal, and from the principal to the teachers. Ultimately, teachers are the doers, but they are often the furthest removed from the decision-making table. When rolling out campus initiatives or embarking on the change process, it is important to have teachers sitting at the table. Allow them to be part of the conversation. Listen to their suggestions, concerns, hopes, and fears. This discourse will help leaders think through the change process and make more informed decisions that impact the lives of the teachers on the campus.

I often hear leaders talk about the importance of buy-in when implementing change within an organization. I have never been one to subscribe to this theory. In fact, I don't seek buy-in at all. Some decisions must be made for various reasons. Not all decisions are able to be made collaboratively; however, when this is the case, it is important for teachers to understand the why behind the decisions that were made. When the why is explicitly stated, in a manner that validates teacher concerns, and the leader creates conditions to support teachers through the implementation process, teacher voice is respected.

When implementing any change initiative, I prefer ownership over buy-in. Initiatives that are implemented through the buy-in process will likely fade away when the leader who implemented the change leaves the organization. Buy-in is often

earned because of position and the power of convincing. Ownership is created through the shared decision-making process that
is grounded in professionalism and mutual respect. Getting to
ownership is a process that is gained through building authentic
relationships that honor and respect teacher voice.

Nothing amplifies teacher voice more than a conversation.
If we truly value the professional thoughts and opinions of our
teachers, we should engage in authentic conversations about
the work. One of the ways I seek to respect teacher voice on
my campus is through one-on-one chats with teacher leaders.
These talks have an open agenda and I encourage authentic
conversation, which includes topics that might be difficult to
discuss. If I don't model that I am open to being put in vulnerable situations, how will I ever get teachers to the level of
ownership that is needed to support and sustain change initiatives. In addition to one-on-one chats, I also meet with grade
level teams. Again, these meetings do not involve a structured
agenda. I start by stating that the meeting belongs to the team.
I ask if there are any concerns, wants, or wishes. I take notes
as I actively listen to what is being shared. I do my best not
to give reasons or explanations unless I am asked to do so. I
take the information and seek to solve the issue, if a solution
is needed, and I also reflect on how I can improve the way I
communicate as a leader.

One of the most beneficial outcomes to these quarterly team
chats is the relationship building that naturally happens during the meeting. Once teachers share their burning issues, the
rest of the time gives us the opportunity to learn more about
each other personally. One of my favorite sayings is that people
don't care how much you know until they know how much
you care. Teachers don't care about the initiatives and agendas
of school leaders until the initiatives and agendas are owned
collectively; and more importantly, teachers must feel that the
leader cares about them on a personal level. We have to rehu-
manize our profession and remember that our job as a leader
is to serve those who, in most cases, had no choice in choosing
the leader they are expected to follow. This is very humbling.
I can't expect teachers to follow and implement my "bright

ideas" and execute the vision I have for our school if I don't allow them to be a part of the process in the development and execution of those ideas.

Another important strategy that has worked for me is saying yes more than I say no. There are many aspects of schooling where teachers do not have a say in what happens in public education. Giving teachers permission to work through the parameters that have been set is possible if the leader has developed a collaborative culture that values shared decision making. Shared decision making leads to a culture where teachers understand the big picture.

Lastly, I constantly gather feedback through open-ended surveys and informal settings. Not all teachers feel comfortable talking in a group. Open-ended surveys give teachers the opportunity to share in a safe space. During my second principalship, I told my staff that I was going on a listening tour when I shared my entry plan with them. On this listening tour I asked more questions than I provided answers, which took a great deal of restraint. Asking the why behind initiatives that were put in place before I transitioned to the campus helped me to see if individuals within the organization were committed to the initiative through the ownership process or if they were just borrowing the implementation as a buy-in participant. What I learned is that the initiatives that involved teacher voice during the creation process garnered more commitment and collective ownership. Teachers were engaged in this work and constantly desired to get better and grow in this learning.

If leaders want to authentically engage teachers by amplifying their voice, they have to make themselves available, accessible, and vulnerable to engage in dialogue that is meaningful and purposeful.

## Focus on Feedback

One evening, when I was preparing dinner for my family, my 8-year-old daughter, Paige, wanted to show me the progress she had made on a series of gymnastics moves she was working on perfecting. I stepped away from the kitchen to watch her perform. Prior to beginning her routine, she asked me to video her demonstration. At the conclusion of her one-woman show, I applauded her performance and asked her the following question, "Why did you want me to record your performance?" She responded, "I wanted to see myself so that I [will know what I] can keep working on and practicing." She felt safe to perform in front of me and cared enough about my opinion to ask me what I thought about her performance. She wanted feedback from a person she respected because she knows that I care about and support her.

This scenario easily transfers to the educational setting between leaders and teachers. Teachers perform multiple times a day in an isolated environment. How often do teachers really receive feedback that leads to meaningful engagement? I am not speaking to the obligatory evaluations that must be completed to fulfill a compliance component. I am referring to feedback that engages teachers throughout the entire process. For example, before I enter a teacher's classroom for a formal evaluation, I ask them if there is something they want me to give them specific feedback about as it relates to their professional practice. I seek to give them support in the growth spots they have identified professionally. Giving quality feedback, in a supportive learning and working environment, makes the impossibles become possible.

As a former basketball coach, I find that some of my coaching principles have transferred naturally to my role as a leader. Before each practice, I created a practice plan that outlined all of the skills I was going to focus on developing during practice. I always made time for individual and group skill work, which allowed me to work with my players on a more personal and direct level. During our basketball games, whenever I noticed that the team or an individual was struggling to execute the game plan, I called a timeout to reset, remind, and refocus the team. As a coach, I focused on player development as well as the collective efficacy of the team. I felt that if I gave each player the right feedback and time to practice, I would be able to help them grow individually, which would ultimately help the entire team.

The scenario just described is analogous to what the relationship between a leader and a teacher should look like. Teachers should receive timely, specific, just-in-time feedback that is given in a way that helps them reflect on their practice. When I was an elementary principal, I worked with a committed team of teachers. Although they were on various levels professionally, I felt that I could help each one of them grow by providing the right feedback and support. The majority of the staff had at least 5–15 years of experience, and a handful of them were fairly new to the profession. If some of the teachers were surveyed by the Gallup instrument, I would guess that some would have been classified as being engaged. These teachers were compliant, dependable, and open to feedback that would help them get better, but they didn't necessarily seek out the feedback because they felt that everything was "just fine." I did, however, have a handful of teachers who were actively engaged. They were on fire for the profession and exuded passion. These teachers fueled my excitement as a leader, and I loved being in their presence. I wanted every teacher to experience active engagement. I knew that if they tasted that level of engagement, the professional capital in our building would increase exponentially, but more importantly, students would ultimately benefit.

As part of my leadership growth, I selected two teachers, unbeknownst to them, to practice my belief about how feedback leads to increased engagement. Both teachers were within their first five years of teaching. I would consider one teacher as engaged and the other teacher as actively engaged.

I asked both teachers, in an informal setting, what areas were they focusing on growing professionally and what support they needed from me through this process. When I visited their classrooms I took notes, which served as a running record for the growth I witnessed throughout the school year, and I provided specific feedback after each visit. I also shared articles, blogs, and other resources that I thought would be of interest to them. I was absolutely amazed at the level of growth and engagement that I observed from the teacher I had classified as engaged at the beginning of the year. In fact, this teacher moved from being lukewarm to being on fire! It was a definite leadership win for me because I felt that really spending time learning the needs of this teacher helped me to focus on how I could support her growth. It also pushed me professionally because I had to redefine what I wanted my leadership to look like on a daily basis. I wanted to coach. I wanted to help others grow in ways that they didn't even know was possible. Below is a message I received from the teacher described above:

> I am reaching out to you because I need your help. This year has been a wonderful whirlwind and such a growing experience for me as an educator. When you left, I felt as though I was beginning to break through the settling first years and was discovering my inner confidence and craft. Honestly, I attribute much of this growth to your leadership; constantly pushing us to go outside of our comfort zones and that the best lesson learned is the way in which we overcome from our failures.

This email came out of the blue and after I had left the school. I don't share this to boast, but as an example of how feedback can positively impact the level of engagement a teacher experiences. When I read this I felt validated in my beliefs about how authentic feedback contributes to active teacher engagement. I think it clearly illustrates that leaders have significant influence in how teachers engage in their work. Granted, the teacher had to have a desire to engage on another level, but I believe that when a leader models active engagement for teachers, the chances of increased teacher engagement are high. By focusing on each teacher's individual needs, I was able to remove the labels that teachers are often given to describe their level of proficiency. Teachers then become learners who are seeking to grow instead of being seen as emerging, proficient, or master teachers.

## Supporting the Whole Teacher

Being a leader is a huge responsibility. Teachers, students, and parents are watching your every move. People want to know what makes you tick as a person, and it matters to them what you think. Because of my position as a leader, I recognize that I have a responsibility to the people I serve each day. Although there are days that I fall short, I seek to add value to someone's life each day. I am not perfect by any means, and unfortunately, I do miss opportunities. When that occurs, I constantly think about what I need to do the next time to correct the missed opportunity to engage with teachers in a meaningful way. If you, as the leader, are not making others who work around you better, then I question your purpose. Leaders must see every single encounter with a teacher as an opportunity for authentic engagement.

By striving to connect with teachers in authentic ways, leaders get to know them on a more personal level. I am very intentional about keeping our relationships on a professional level, but I don't keep teachers at an arm's distance. I have a pretty active social media life that has given me the opportunity to engage with educators from all over the world. Surely the teachers I work with on a daily basis deserve to know me on a deeper level than my social media network. I can't support the whole teacher if I don't know the whole teacher. Teachers do not check their personal baggage at the door when they enter the schoolhouse. They bring their joys, frustrations, burdens, and problems with them each day. Letting teachers know that I care about them as a person is so important. We have to be willing to meet people where they are in order to help and support them on the journey of becoming what they desire to be.

Being intentional about showing teachers appreciation throughout the school year is also a contributing factor to increasing teacher engagement. I am not speaking of the traditional times of the year when leaders are told to appreciate teachers (e.g. Teacher Appreciation Week), but the other 170 days when teachers are doing their best to reach each individual child. I must be honest, this is an area where I have to continue to grow. This is not something I inherently think about doing, but I do recognize the importance of showing appreciation even in the smallest ways.

While writing this chapter, I took a brain break and shared where I was in the writing process with Bob Dillon. As we were talking, he asked me, "What's your third place?" I had no idea how to answer his question. He went on to explain that everyone has a first, second, and third place. First place is home, family, personal life, etc. Second place is work responsibilities and third place refers to the activities and hobbies that serve as a release from personal and professional responsibilities. Supporting the whole teacher means recognizing the multifaceted lives they lead and encouraging them to find a balance between these places. Although most educators consider their work to be their calling, it should not consume their life. Overcommitment and being stretched too thin does not lead to active engagement; it leads to burnout. Modeling balance as leaders gives teachers permission to practice this strategy as well.

## Read, Write, Action

Leaders must be able and willing to help teachers connect their why to the work. This activity can give new meaning and redefine the purpose for each individual. Being able to anchor the work to a greater purpose is what will sustain and motivate teachers through challenges. In addition, when teachers are a part of creating the purpose of the organization, the long-term benefits of ownership will carry the organization further along than the short-term wins that buy-in promises. Furthermore, leaders must be intentional about developing a culture that promotes, encourages, and cultivates learning by giving teachers the opportunity to learn from one another. Encouraging this type of collaboration will not only build the professional capital of the teachers, but also deepen and enrich the collegial collaboration amongst them as well. When teachers know that they are appreciated, valued, and supported in all aspects of their lives, they will be committed to their work and to those around them. This commitment will fuel them with the desire to become better each day.

Although leadership is not the only gatekeeper to teacher engagement, it is certainly a critical component to creating an environment that fosters active engagement. Leaders must be willing to change the way they think about their responsibility in cultivating a working environment that promotes and supports active engagement. It has been my personal experience that strong leadership is a contributing factor to building a positive, engaging working environment for teachers. In the absence of leadership, only pockets of excellence will exist, but with strong leaders at the helm, systems of excellence that foster and support high teacher engagement can be created and sustained.

## References

www.gallup.com/services/180029/gallup-student-poll-2014-overall-report.aspx

https://www.ted.com/talks/simon_sinek_how_great_leaders_inspire_action

Busteed, B. (2015). The magical elements of college linked to long-term success in work and life. *About Campus*,19(6), 2–8.

# 8

# Changing the Way We Think About Leadership

Amber Teamann

This chapter is dedicated to the memory of my uncle, Freddy Nugent.

The word "administrator" can often have a negative connotation. It's the person you see when you are in trouble, the stern non-smiling face, the one who makes all of the decisions. The administrator is the one who writes up the teachers, delivers the evaluations, and is potentially the holder of all the jobs. I often comment that everyone laughs at my jokes, but that doesn't actually guarantee that they are funny. When I walk into the room, people sit up a little straighter and the personal chatter quiets. Questions are answered in the way that the room thinks I want to hear versus what they may actually be thinking. My position now precedes my person. People aren't talking to *me*, they are talking to the boss, and it influences every single one of our interactions. Culture was impacted because of the inauthenticity . . . and as the principal, I was missing any indicator that there was something amiss.

## Administrator as the Scapegoat

There was a **letter** recently that went viral on Facebook criticizing an administrator's upholding of a dress code requirement.

Her daughter was at a stage where her long legs meant the shorts expectation was difficult to shop for. The mother lamented against the policy of the shorts length . . . and it was directed at the principal. Odds are incredibly high that the principal under attack had nothing to do with the actual creation of that dress code, but was still the lead villain in the public eye. **Why is the administrator always the bad guy?**

In 2015 Mike Rossi wrote a scathing response to his principal who "criticized" him for taking his kids out of school to see him run the Boston Marathon and pay tribute to the bombing victims. The criticism that was his catalyst? An automated letter to inform the parents of potential academic consequences if there were too many unexcused absences. Again, the principal was to blame. She received *death threats* over an automated form letter, which she was required by law to send. **Why is the administrator always the bad guy?**

Recently I read the New York Times article "Want to Fix Schools? Go to the Principal's Office", and again was struck by the tone that reflected negatively on the role of the leader (New York Times, 2017). Pleasing everyone is impossible, and is that really what the goal should be? Student centered, teacher supportive, parent pleasing, while maintaining academic integrity, but also lead innovative change and challenge the status quo . . . there is no winning! The principal helps set the culture which helps retain teachers, yes, but why is the onus not on the system in which we operate? The brief "Musical Chairs: Teacher Churn and Its impact on Indianapolis Public Schools," published by Teach Plus (Teach Plus, n.d.), stated: "for teachers who voluntarily left a school at some point in their career, 49 percent cited school leadership and 40 percent cited school culture as reasons for leaving." **Why is the administrator always the bad guy?**

Recognizing that our chosen title and role is typically viewed through an accusatory lens means going into every situation focused not on how to be right, but on how to value the relationship. At the end of the day, regardless of how "right" you are, if you've damaged the trust and safety that allows for an honest conversation, you've actually made less progress than your rightness is worth. Perception can become reality. Valuing the perspectives of both staff and families in that manner requires a balance of wanting to meet everyone's needs while maintaining the vision and success of *all* facets within your building. Misreading or mishandling even a minor conversation can allow a crack in the foundation of what, ultimately, we are trying to accomplish. We can't control the negativity, but we can control our reaction and how that impacts the overall school culture.

## Developing Emotional Intelligence to Lead

Knowing that unpopular decisions are part of the responsibility of being the administrator comes with is recognizing that we are the ones who control the temperature. Recently we were potentially going to add a seventh 4th grade section at our school. We were already bursting with 50 more students in that grade level than in any other. When I let the team know that adding a new section was a possibility, they immediately went into overdrive. Where to put them, how to team them, who to even hire to teach them? I didn't react, I reassured. I calmly redirected their time and energy into planning for what was already in place. I was quite confident in sharing that it probably wasn't going to happen, and that we would be fine. It was almost like someone let the air out of a balloon. They immediately took deep breaths and calmed down. My assistant principal literally said, "If Teamann's not worried, I'm not worried." I was amazed.

It sounds so commonsensical, but they looked to *me* to see how *they* should react. If I am calm, they are calm. If I am upset, they get upset. Think of how powerful our role is . . . you are not the thermometer, but you absolutely have the power to set the thermostat as the leader in your building. Use that power for good! Having a high **emotional intelligence** (EI) requires being able to connect in a genuine manner in order to make decisions and move a campus or district forward. To be effective, leaders must have a solid understanding of how their emotions and actions affect the people around them. The better an administrator relates to and works with others, the more successful s/he will be. According to Daniel Goleman (Goleman, 2004), an American psychologist who helped to popularize emotional intelligence, there are five key elements:

1. Self-awareness
2. Self-regulation
3. Motivation
4. Empathy
5. Social skills

My first year as principal, I neglected to evaluate my EI and the campus culture struggled because of it. Not recognizing the signs of tacit disagreement meant I missed what was happening in the subculture of my building. The result? Unhappy teachers and unhappy parents. Definitely not my goal!

How then did I turn that around? Slowing down. Asking questions rather than making decisions. Recognizing that 95% of the decisions made didn't require an immediate answer allowed me to process more slowly and take the time to find a right answer versus an immediate answer. As someone once told me, "No one bleeds to death on our watch."

We are fortunate enough to have positions that are incredibly important and impactful but that don't require an instantaneous decision/response in most cases. Taking the time to have conversations with your staff builds trust and allows a collaborative style of leadership that garners not only support, but also ensures input. If a leader is unable to make decisions based on the feedback gathered, who is benefiting? Not the staff, not the students, and certainly not the leader.

### Changing the Way We Look at What Leaders Do

The administration title carries with it a unique workload. Our days are filled with decisions. From decisions that have a major impact to decisions that have a minor impact, we spend each day with a list of things to do, and then chase the many fires that occur instead. We know the good, the bad, and the ugly . . . from students to staff, to our community. On any given day we decide everything ranging from what goes in a coke machine to whether we feel a parent is mistreating a child.

Much of what we do is dictated by state and district policy, yet there is no instruction manual provided when named "administrator." When we are able to make a sustainable impact, we are still held to the highest of expectations. That's why we get the big bucks, right? To never make mistakes and ensure that everyone is happy. Our decisions and the implications of what we say goes is a heavy load to bear. It's an incredible honor, but it's also incredibly stressful. There literally is no winning in some situations. Not everyone will be happy with the decisions made. Leadership means making the hard decisions sometimes. Recognizing that education itself is different than it was even just 10–20 years ago calls for also recognizing that the way we look at the role of "administrator" needs to change. It needs to evolve before any other changes we want to see happen in education can occur because—like with most other decisions made in a school—it starts and can stop right at our door.

## Leading With Relational Purpose

When I think of administrators in my own education experience, I can recall faces. I don't remember most of their names, and I definitely don't remember interacting with any of them. As a student, I don't remember them in my classroom. As a teacher, I don't recall my superintendent or principal hanging out in my classroom. As a parent, our interactions have been perfunctory . . . congenial, yes, but not personal. Traditionally, principals stay in their offices, and handle the "bad" kids, the "difficult" parents. They are also frequently in meetings. They are not instructional leaders. They are responsible for completing a minimum number of classroom walk-throughs and teacher evaluations. Teaching strategies or instructional best practices are up to the teacher to find and implement. The ineffective administrator holds staff meetings that could have been emails, and is always looking for the "gotcha" moment. They aren't "friends" with their staff and aren't seen outside the school walls interacting with the staff/community. They are feared, rather than respected or followed. An ineffective principal works alone, in a silo, and is inflexible in what and how things are done. They are autocratic leaders, isolated from input or support. They make choices based on their ideas and judgments and rarely accept advice from their staff or anyone around them. Test results/data are dissected, with little to no direction on how to improve, other than the directive *to* improve. **The words "We've always done it this way" is their mantra**. Worse yet, they have no problems with how they are doing things, especially if there is a modicum of success to support what they are doing. If parents and staff aren't unhappy, if test scores aren't abysmal, there is no impetus for change.

Knowing that this is not the leadership style I want to emulate, the intentionality placed on relationship building in my world is tantamount to my success as a leader and our success as a school. Academic success and student growth is the given, but we can—and should—do more for our students. Increasing the capacity of our teachers to stretch beyond the walls of their classrooms, to build genuine caring relationships with our students and parents, while administrators are modeling the same thing . . . there is no end to what we can accomplish together.

Gone are the days where anyone can do this job alone. A quote that anchors much of what I believe and share is by David Weinberger, who suggests that the smartest person in the room is not any one person, but the room itself (Weinberger, 2014). Connecting to other practitioners today is too easy for it to not be happening in school districts and campuses worldwide. Whether it's a virtual relationship via social media, or a core group of local peers whose opinions you value, there is so much benefit in having a group to collaborate or share ideas with. It can also be lonely in that office all by yourself. By developing relationships and making professional connections, you are exponentially increasing your ability and opportunity for success within your walls. By flattening what we think of when we think "administrator," we have the power to change everything about what we do. An administrator who dares to do things differently and challenge the status quo can not only transform their own role, but also empower all of those with whom they serve . . . by bringing them alongside.

## Doing It Differently

This year I've had the chance to work closely with a parent at our campus. Her special needs son would be attending our school, as his brothers had before him. Her family had an incredible history with our campus, which predated my tenure there. The campus was there for her when they discovered she was expecting. They were there for her when she found out she having her first little girl. They were also there when she delivered not a little girl, but a boy. A boy with Down syndrome. When we met to discuss his placement, it became obvious that a "what we had always done" answer wasn't going to work for her. A self-contained classroom wasn't what she wanted, and I couldn't guarantee it was what he needed. She wanted him to experience what his brothers had experienced before him . . . and why shouldn't he be able to? From the very beginning, my goal was simple. I wanted to do what was best for Levi. Not a child with Down's . . . but Levi. We were willing to do something different in order to see what we could make work for her son. For Levi. I stressed to her over and over that I wasn't sure what this would look like, how we would make this work, but that we were going to keep trying until we got it right. We had many, many meetings. There were many, many calls. Days where his teacher was in tears, days where his momma was in tears, days where her principal was in tears. We kept trying. By the end of the year, through the efforts of everyone working together we found a balance that met his needs—*Levi's* needs.

The relationship that this family and I now have is what I consider a "normal" parent relationship for the type of leader I want to be. I've watched him play buddy ball on Saturday morning, I've chased him around the playground. His teacher is incredibly proud of how far he has come, socially and academically. She'd be the first to tell you that he changed the dynamics of her classroom. There have been afternoons of long conversations and awkward silences. It has required more processing and trying different things, but it has allowed us to truly evaluate what he needs, rather than a set of accommodations that are automatically assumed. I write him postcards commending his progress in class and he feeds me a goldfish cracker at lunch when I see him. Our selfie count is in the double digits. His mother and I have innumerable conversations, some more tense than others, she with her mom hat on and I with my administrator hat on. I've told her that she is the one who will fight for Levi as her son and I am the one who will fight for Levi as a learner. Those aren't mutually exclusive, and we're OK with it. There are no "what we've always done" in this situation, and I can't tell you how proud that makes me of our school.

## Flattening the Role of Administrator

One of my goals as an administrator is to flatten the role. I want staff and families to *remember* who I am and the impact I had on our campus. I can't do that from within my office. That doesn't mean I don't get my campus improvement plan written or handle the budget and offer managerial matters; it means I am very strategic in the things I do in order to build a relationship. Second grade teacher Kayla Delzer said during her TEDx (YouTube, n.d.) talk that "relationships between students and passionate teachers will always be the foundation of successful classrooms," and I think that applies to every level of administration in our educational system. We need *passionate* superintendents, directors of curriculum, teachers, secretaries, etc. If you work with students, you must be passionate about what you do, because it all matters. The connections that each role can have on the trajectory of a child can never be understated.

My daughter played both volleyball and basketball in junior high and was relatively good at both sports. Before her freshman year she attended a basketball camp at the high school and had a passing conversation with the new incoming varsity girls coach. He stopped and watched her play for a bit. As they chatted afterwards he mentioned he saw something in her playing and was looking forward to working with her in the next few years. She came home that day with a new energy and focus towards basketball. She ended up dropping volleyball, so she could focus solely on basketball. That changed her schedule . . . her group of athletic friends . . . her entire plan for her freshman year changed based on a passing conversation and the words "I see something in you." We can't underestimate the power we have in our words, and as an administrator, it is we who model and empower those who work with us to be different.

I am fortunate enough to work in a district that supports the power of relationships and the ways they are developed. We have a large presence on social media, so there's no shying away from who we are and what we do. My superintendent takes selfies with kids daily, and on the first day of school he visits every school and shares how smoothly things are going. Do you know how reassuring that is to our community? His boots are on the ground . . . he's taking pictures within our halls, not just telling people what he thinks is happening in our district. He is a proud Texas Tech Red Raider and on each campus he visits he hands out a dollar bill to the first person who sees him and gives him the "Guns up!" hand symbol associated with his university. One could take that just as a relationship-building piece, but extrapolate it further. He is recognized and celebrated when seen. Students *flock* to him . . . they know where he went to college, acknowledge it, and are able to give him the "Guns Up!" sign, which is the widely recognized greeting of one Red Raider to another. It is also the sign of victory displayed by the crowd at every athletic event. What an incredible way to support a love of tradition and collegiate awareness!

Flattening the role of administrator means doing things in a new way. Several years ago the conversation centered around social media and for many educators this was a scary one. Don't do it, you can get fired, don't put yourself out there. That is still a prevalent thought in some circles. Not only am I active on multiple social media platforms, I don't shy away from my love of what I do, or how proud I am of our students and staff. This serves so many purposes. First, I try to be a model for others of what a positive, appropriate online presence can look like. I don't use my platform to complain or vent. Early on I was given the advice that the only things I should post, ever, are things that I would be OK with being on the front page of the newspaper. Second, by friending those I professionally connect myself to, I am able to collaborate with like-minded peers. Ideas, suggestions, catalysts for greatness . . . all at my fingertips. Third, amplifying all that I see and am proud of empowers my staff and students to know that there is an authentic audience viewing what we are trying to accomplish. We crowdsourced and chose a hashtag to help unify what we were sharing. Part of flattening our roles is recognizing that we have to be in control of what story we're telling. Each share made with the #wearewhitt hashtag is a sentence in our story. One of student voice, teacher empowerment, staff dedication, and parent commitment. In the same way you can read my blog and know what I stand for, the same can be said for our #wearewhitt messages.

Last, I want people to know who I am, and what I stand for. While in my administrative role, I strive to not make campus decisions based solely on what I believe in or think are best practices. I ask questions and seek to bring them forward. The goal as the leader should be to empower each of them to be the very best version of themselves that they can be. Whether they walk, crawl, or run, we all are moving forward, together. The campus isn't solely there to execute all my ideas of grandeur.

When you read my blog or see the conversations I have on Twitter, you know what I believe. My thoughts are my own and the reflections of my journey are documented and very public. I speak nationally on what digital leadership means and what our responsibilities represent to the students we serve. That power is not taken lightly. The benefit of having it out there is that should my people choose to follow or friend me, they get to *know* me. The more transparent I am the more my people get to know me as Amber, and not as "the principal." Changing the way we look at leadership means that instead of only seeing the title or the role, we see and know the person. I am a mother, a wife, a daughter. Someone with friends and professional goals . . . who makes mistakes, but strives to not make the same mistake twice. Someone who wants what it is that I want evidenced through my digital footprint. The more transparent you are, the more people feel like they know you, and are more likely to want to connect with you. I want to be seen as approachable, as someone they can come talk to and share with if needed.

## Developing Your Vision for a Changed Leadership

Building a family atmosphere is a focus each year at our school. An inordinate amount of time is spent in developing professional development for our staff each year. There is a theme, and down to the color of the pens at the table, each decision is made with the intent of conveying our message. Having a teenager in my house means that I've seen the *Hunger Games* a ridiculous amount of times. One time after it had played and she'd left the room, it went into the "director's cut" portion of the DVD. When the director got the script he immediately locked himself in a room and wrote out every possible thought he had on what he wanted to see happen in the film. There were costuming notes, there were set details, there were very minute thoughts written out. The purpose of this was genius. While filming there would be many questions asked in the crux of the moment and he didn't want to allow any of those questions to be answered based on what was easiest in the moment. What he envisioned and wanted to "see" might be more complicated, but to ensure that was what was done, he wrote it out. Costume managers said that his vision was so clear that when they had a question they didn't have to rely on what they thought he wanted, but could reference back to that script he'd added to and know they were keeping up with his wishes.

Your vision for your campus should permeate every decision you make. If you are relationship focused, that should be reflected in what you say, what you share, and how you come across. Each year, I want to send every single one of my students a postcard, telling them how proud of them I am, and that I am thankful they are Whitt Wolves. With 670 kids, this is not something I can put off or think I can rush through at the end of the year. Each week I ask teachers to share someone from their class they are proud of, and I am able to send a brief note. Time to write these cards is on my calendar and I make it a priority to get them done. From allocating additional money in my budget for materials to the time set aside on my calendar, that this is important to me is reflected in those decisions.

Selfies with students that are sent home to parents is another way to connect and build relationships. Modeling for students what we share and say online covers two bases. It not only makes them feel special for that moment, but when parents are able to ask specifically about what they saw on our social media channels, we're letting in the parents who aren't able to be there each day. From celebrating an academic success to highlighting a Dallas Cowboys shirt, parents and our community know what we are doing each day. The "what did you do today?" question is answered differently when you can say, "I saw you building a robot in science, what was that all about?" I love that my teachers are able to sneak in our high expectations and the excellence that we see through sharing with our families. Each teacher has a protected account via a form of social media that allows them to personally connect. Gone are the days of the weekly newsletter that may or may not be read in the go-home folder; we communicate, remind, and share *daily*.

## Changing the Way You Think of Teacher Leaders

Empowering teachers is one of the most important things an administrator can do. While it may be easy to just move along teachers who don't mesh with your vision, it can also be because they aren't allowed to be successful with their strengths. Do you know the strengths of your team? Through the Gallup organization evaluation, my number one strength is as an activator. Gallup defines an activator as "the ones who make things happen. One of their most recognizable behaviors is the ability to turn thoughts, ideas and concepts into action. In fact, the strength of Activator can be best described or characterized as action." Thankfully my assistant principal has the strength of being a **processor**, which means she moves slowly and deliberately. I move her forward and she slows me down. When making decisions this presents a strong balance, and we are all better for it!

When thinking about the strengths of our teachers, we've tried to balance along the same lines. We have one teacher who could be thought of as negative because she asks a ton of questions about everything, from details to timelines; from the outside it would appear as if she is trying to poke holes in what we are trying to achieve. After learning that her strength is **consistency**, it made so much more sense! Now she is one of the first people we go to with a plan or an idea, because she helps shore it up and makes it stronger, and more complete. Knowing that her intent was to understand clearly and see all the details helped me value the voice she brought to the table. She is more confident in her opinions and questions now, where before she may have been hesitant to share with the whole group. We've helped others see and appreciate what her purpose is in speaking out.

## Bringing It All Together

All administrators have the same amount of hours in the day. There are a myriad of responsibilities that we are tasked with overseeing. At the forefront of what we all want to accomplish is the notion that the buck stops with us. If leaders lead they way they've always done, it will be next to impossible to see sweeping change through the educational system. No longer is isolation an option, nor should we feel like sharing allows others to get ahead of where we want to be. **Educational leadership is not a zero-sum game**. Zero-sum is a situation in game theory in which one person's gain is equivalent to another's loss, so the net change in wealth or benefit is zero. Success of one child is a success for all children. Teachers that are taking risks and stepping out of the traditional role should be lauded for their initiative instead of being told to stay in their lane. Administrators should be comfortable going to conferences, learning from people who are doing things in an unfamiliar way. Confident leadership models that there is always a different way of doing something, and that one doesn't ever stop learning.

# References

https://www.nytimes.com/2017/03/10/opinion/sunday/want-to-fix-schools-go-to-the-principals-office.html

http://teachplus.org/news-events/publications/musical-chairs-teacher-churn-and-its-impact-indianapolis-public-schools

Goleman, D. (2004). Emotional Intelligence; Working with Emotional Intelligence. London: Bloomsbury.

Weinberger, D. (2014). Too Big to Know: Rethinking Knowledge now That the Facts Arent the Facts, Experts are Everywhere. New York: Basic Books.

https://www.youtube.com/watch?v=w6vVXmwYvgs

# 9

# Changing the Way We Think About Partnerships

## Bob Dillon

This chapter is dedicated to Matt and Matt, two beautiful humans who ended their lives too soon.

As we move from a time when it takes a village to support all children to a time when it takes a global village and deep partnerships to do the same work, it is essential that we begin to shift the understanding of what it means to partner with schools in ways that create a genuine modern community around students and adult learners.

Many schools are pursuing new and different community partnerships to support their modern learning environments. In some places, these are emerging out of strengths as resources in the community are entering the district to both supplement and supplant the status quo. They are also surrounding good and excellent programming to give students additional experiences and opportunities. In other locations, partnership development is coming as a result of shrinking budgets and the need to supplement classroom teaching because of teacher shortages or lack of supplies.

We are in a time when it takes a cohort of educators and partners to bring the rich learning experiences that kids need. It is essential that all classrooms, schools, and districts continue to look at community partnerships as a way to bring modern learning experiences to all kids. Seeking these partnerships is the right and moral thing to do for all our students as the learning outcomes that we seek grow more and more complex.

## Home Visits

Starting a journey together on common ground allows for a different type of trust. It allows for smiles to be shared, and it allows for the journey to be based on strengths. It is in these concepts that home visits were based at Saint Louis Public Schools (MO). They recognized that it would take time and resources in the summer, but they felt that the time spent up front would lead to amazing payoffs.

Through this work, teachers were welcomed into home after home for conversations about the beauty and strengths of incoming students. These conversations were positive in energy, and they focused on listening to the needs of the family. The visits were designed to reach out to mothers, fathers, grandparents, and guardians who may not have experienced school in a positive way or potentially had moments of harm during their time in the classroom. Home visits were designed to reset the conversation, and start a relationship. They were focused on everyone working together to bring growth to the student.

Home visits became a central tenet of the philosophy at Saint Louis Public Schools to reshape the way that community partnerships were taking place. Word quickly spread that teachers and principals wanted to be in the community growing their understanding and seeking a relationship with students and their families.

The true power of this work comes from being in the homes of students. Within these spaces, teachers meet family partners who are seeking the support of the school to make sure their child can be truly successful. All parents can be willing partners. Sometimes parents will share during these home visits about previous educators and schools that failed to make the connection that the home visit was providing and how it leaves many parents locked out of the system. Years later, home visits continue to have power. Parents will stop educators to remind them of that night when the home visit team knocked on the door and started the work needed for their child to succeed.

Though no formal program is needed to have successful home visits, the Saint Louis Public Schools program was a layered community partnership that included the support of a Saint Louis-based organization called *Home Works! The Teacher Home Visit Program*. *Home Works!* trains and helps pay teachers and other school personnel to make home visits to forge a relationship with the parents/families/guardians and get them engaged in their child's education. Teachers get to know them, share information about the student, and give them the tools to help children do better in school and succeed academically and socially. They use two different models to get their results: the *2+2 model* and the Parent Teacher Learning Team Model or *PLTL model*.

Schools looking to change the way that they think about community partnership would be wise to inquire about how to bring home visits to their schools in a meaningful, systemic way. It opens the lines of communication and humanizes the learning process.

Consider these resources as a way to begin the conversation about home visits in your schools (see information for finding these resources at the end of this chapter):

- *Parent Teacher Home Visits-*

## Arts Integration

Learning weaved through the head and heart allows for a stickiness needed at a time when the information noise that surrounds all students is growing. It is when we look for ways to bring the arts into learning that we find a new synergy and a fresh energy to surround the learning of all kids. Arts integration isn't a new concept when it comes to education in general, but most schools still aren't seeking deep community partnerships to bring arts integration to a new level.

As our digital connections grow, the opportunity to bring artists into the classroom to support and partner in learning continues to grow. Some communities have a deep artistic tradition in music, visual arts, graphic arts, folk arts, and others. Other communities lack these hyperlocal connections, but instead they can now reach authors, artists, and musicians and loop them into conversations, projects, and mentorships as students embark on arts integrated projects through technology.

One example of this work in action comes from the Integrated Arts Academy at H.O. Wheeler in Burlington, VT. This school has a rich tradition of embedding the arts as a cornerstone to the learning experience for students. Students learn through the lens of the four art forms: movement, drama, music, and visual arts, and they work in partnership with The Flynn Center for Performing Arts, St. Michael's College, Burlington City Arts, Champlain College, and the Boys and Girls Club of Burlington.

Integrating a bevy of partnerships together can often be the challenge for many schools as partnership maintenance can rival partnership development. Partnership by design should be a two-way street where the partner sees their work with the school as a growth opportunity for the business or organization as well. Business partners can gain insight about school age interest, adding energy to their place of work, and potentially get fresh ideas and solutions to incorporate. This is a shift in thinking for many community partners because the norm is currently community giving rather than true partnership.

Another emerging example of community partnership in arts integration comes from The School District of University City in Saint Louis, MO, where they are using their community resources to build an incredible arts integration studio. This community partnership is reclaiming a space that was once a library to become an art studio and gallery. Once completed, it will feature two artists in residence creating and showcasing their creative process. The space will also feature a rotating gallery of students and community artwork. Throughout the school day, it will also be a learning studio for students with their paints and supplies filling the room. The final piece to this arts integration space will be a "blackbox" presentation space for students to showcase their work as well as get feedback from classmates and community members.

Weaving the arts into learning doesn't have to be an every-lesson, every-unit situation, but it continues to make sense to triangulate the ways that we make learning meaningful, fun, and engaging. Using the arts as a way of making this a reality will continue to be a part of the recipe for leaders looking to link community to school.

Consider these resources as a way to begin the conversation about arts integration as a philosophy for community engagement (see information for finding these resources at the end of this chapter):

- *Learning In and Through the Arts*
- *Arts Integration: The Kennedy Center's Perspective*
- *Teachers and Teaching Artists as Agents of Change*
- *Arts Integration: New Research on Effective Practice, Sustainability, and the Role of Teachers and Teaching Artists*

## Building Community Advocates

Our schools are our communities, and our communities are our schools. This interconnected reality makes it essential that we lean into the strengths of our community as opposed to sheltering our students from its weaknesses. In doing so, it is quickly unearthed that today's students will play a role in the long-term sustainability of the vitality of any community.

Growing sustainable communities through deep school partnerships can result in growing a more just community in a number of ways. Student voices can speak to the social justice needs of the community. Preparing students for the job needs of the local community supports the economic justice needs of the community, and this often grows a student's sense of place where they are more compelled to support and be an active community member for many years. Having students involved with conversations around sustainable communities also brings a host of environmental justice issues to the table.

All of these conversations and interactions between the schools and community supports growth and stability. It also promotes new ideas and fresh solutions. Building this type of culture and mindset requires schools and districts to begin early. Kindergarten students can be thinking about sustainability at their developmental level, so that as high school students they can be implementing solutions in the community.

Schools that have seen the power of engaging the community through sustainability have often turned to the Education for Sustainability standards. These standards feature nine indicators that can be used to seek out partnerships, plan community-centric work, and focus classrooms on connecting to people, place, and planet. The nine standards are: Cultural Preservation & Transformation, Responsible Local & Global Citizenship, The Dynamics of Systems & Change, Sustainable Economics, Healthy Commons, Natural Laws & Ecological Principles, Inventing & Affecting the Future, Multiple Perspectives, and Strong Sense of Place. More details can be found at The Cloud Institute (The Cloud Institute, n.d.) including crosswalks to Common Core Standards and many other standards.

The State of Washington has engaged community partners for years in the area of sustainability education. Students at Cle Elum Schools conducted a citizen science project that allowed students to contribute to an amazing team of scientists that were looking to complete an area biodiversity inventory. The students gathered data weekly and shared results. This citizen science project and others around the country allow students to engage with community and global studies that can potentially change their community for generations to come.

The conversations needed to sustain communities will require all voices at the table. It will require a partnership between students, leaders, and advocates for change. It will require a "commons" mindset that can only exist in real partnership.

Consider these resources as a way to begin the conversation about education for sustainability as a philosophy for community engagement (see information for finding these resources at the end of this chapter):

- *Citizen Science Alliance*
- *Children's Environmental Literacy Foundation*

- *Sustainable Schools Project*
- *Integrated Environmental and Sustainability K–12 Learning Standards*

## Community Digital Space

The global interconnectedness that has been accelerated by digital tools and resources along with the impact of broadband access and mobile connectivity has shifted the concept of community to expand well beyond the school district and township borders to a more tribal schema that organizes around interests and areas of common need. This shift shouldn't be left out of the consideration of modern educators as they embrace new ways of community partnership.

Most students have areas of passion that can be cultivated and developed with a strong community engagement strategy that includes experts, entrepreneurs, and others that deeply care about the subjects that students are learning beyond the learning of everyday school. How can schools help students to build the healthiest, sustainable tribe in support of this natural learning?

This question supports the need for educators to grow their students' understanding of digital community spaces. It means showing students how to look for experts beyond a single search on YouTube or Google. It means showing students ways to triangulate finding information so that they are truly learning from a robust community and not multiple sources that lead back to the same information. It is normalizing writing, video, podcasts, and various other media as potential ways to grow.

One classroom at Millington Central High School in Millington, TN, took on a project designed to support learning and support the community digital space through their creation, design, and expansion of the community Wikipedia page. Wikipedia is a democratic community space. It allows for all to edit and this freedom leads to long-term accuracy and depth to the knowledge base on almost everything.

Wikipedia has a specific rating system for entries, and when students use this information, they can grow as both consumers and producers in the community digital space. This project is only one example of how students are learning to contribute and use the information available in digital spaces to engage with new communities. Projects like *StoryCorps' Great Thanksgiving Listen* also provided students with great ways to use digital tools to engage with the community.

Community, as we have known it, continues to change. This grows the challenge of educators to surround all kids with the resources that they need. Some schools, though, have found ways to bring individuals and tribes into their learning spaces to support the needs of students through the variety of digital tools available.

Consider these resources as a way to begin the conversation about bringing new experts and resources into the school from the larger digital community (see information for finding these resources at the end of this chapter):

- *Digital Community Engagement Through the Internet*
- *Community Partners: Making Student Learning Relevant*
- *Experts in the Classroom*

## Restorative Justice Practices

In a post-Ferguson society, the concept of community partnership has changed. No matter if you live in an extremely diverse community or an extremely homogeneous one, the conversations about social and economic justice are growing as kitchen table conversations. Communities are looking for the words to put to civil conversations around difficult topics, and it is part of an educator's responsibility to help shape and support these conversations.

Restorative practices as a part of the school system have grown in interest and implementation as schools have looked for ways to heal internal and external wounds within their communities. Looking for ways to shift the traditions of discipline and suspension, schools are focusing on teaching instead of punishing. Though the research remains new and inconclusive around some restorative practices, there continues to be a growing body of stories that showcase how restorative practices can heal communities and provide hope for the future.

Schools are now looking for ways to expand the power of restorative circles into the greater community. One program in Gainesville, FL, at the River Phoenix Center for Peacebuilding, is bringing together youth of color and police officers for conversations to foster empathy and understanding. In many cases, this community partnership looks to start conversations that may have never happened in the past between youth and law enforcement. It doesn't believe that it will end distrust, but it can begin to chip away at the system going forward.

Oakland Unified School District (OUSD, n.d.) has been a leader in the country around this work as well. Using a variety of restorative practices and partnerships, they have cut discipline rates, raised achievement, and reduced the need for more intensive community resources in many neighborhoods. More on their plan can be found here.

Building community partners through the use of restorative justice can be difficult work and multilayered in its implementation. It relies on leaders that see systems as inherently unjust or in need of repair. Working on these injustices through restorative practices can be powerful, and these conversations can also be a springboard for larger community change.

Effective long-term partnerships will continue to be a messy uncomfortable process, but it is in this type of process that justice is most often found.

Consider these resources as a way to begin the conversation about how restorative practices can build greater engagement with the community (see information for finding these resources at the end of this chapter):

- *Restorative Justice in U.S. Schools: A Research Review*
- *Changing School Culture: 5 Schools Practicing Restorative Justice*
- *Videos & Films on Restorative Practices in Schools*
- *Restorative Response to Ferguson, NYC, Cleveland*
- *Reducing Harms to Boys and Young Men of Color From Criminal Justice System Involvement*

## Communities by Design

Communities are a set of constructs woven together to meet the needs of all of its members. Successful communities achieve this to a much greater degree, but the concept of the community is that each individual gives up some of their liberties to achieve a more communal success for all. Achieving this success requires laws, systems, processes, procedures, and numerous unwritten norms.

Schools and students can grow and learn through the study of these community-building structures while at the same time use their perspectives, experiences, and desires for the future to shape their community. Finding entry points into these community concepts is an essential role for educators. Students need to see their community as a place that was originally designed and/or currently designed for success. Many are achieving this work through community-centric, real-world, project-based learning that inserts students into the solution making of their communities.

Another layer of this work to partner comes from area businesses that seek to engage, shape, and build by design the community in which they prosper. The business community can showcase their design process in areas such as: building, marketing, transportation, and supply chain. This allows students to understand how to design for success and the common good.

One project that showcases this work occurred between the students at Maplewood Richmond Heights Middle School (MO) (MRHS, 2011) and Chiodini Associates, a local architecture firm. This partnership resulted in a submission for the *Pruitt Igoe Now* design competition. This competition looked for ideas that re-invigorate the abandoned former federal housing project site. *Pruitt Igoe Now* invited ideas from the creative community worldwide—individuals and teams of professional, academic, and student architects—to reimagine the 57 acres on which the Pruitt Igoe housing project was once located. *Here* is the submission from the Maplewood Richmond Heights (MRH, 2011) students and their community partners at Chiodini Associates.

This project allowed students to see that business and civic leaders recognized the collective needs of the community. It showcased how students could have a powerful voice at the table and how essential change was possible through design and structure. Schools need to continue to showcase that there are solutions through the system as opposed to around the system, and community partnerships with a solution-making focus helps students to see the value of civic systems.

Consider these resources as a way to begin the conversation about using the design of the civic and business communities to showcase how change is possible (see information for finding these resources at the end of this chapter):

- *Center for Communities by Design*
- *Community by Design: New Urbanism for Suburbs and Small Communities*
- *Resources for Building Community Partnerships*
- *A How-To Guide for School–Business Partnerships*
- *Toolkit for Building Partnerships Between Schools and Businesses or Organizations Across South Washington County Schools*

## Apprenticeship

Learning a craft or skill under the guidance and support of a master has been a generational gift across all of time. This essential concept of apprenticeship can and should remain at the core of partnerships for schools. The experts in any community hold trapped wisdom, and this wisdom rarely collides with the formal learning process in most schools. Apprenticeship allows for community norms, beliefs, and work ethic to grow from the community to the school as opposed to the genesis of these skills being found in a math or social studies classroom. Apprenticeship is linked to authentic, hard work.

Community surveys about their employment needs often point to a desire for graduates who can work in teams and solve problems. These traits are often best pursued in an authentic place of work as opposed to the classroom setting, which, no matter how real life it is structured, has a hint or more of artificiality. Students working in the community also grows mutual empathy. There is a narrative that schools in the United States aren't producing excellent students, and worse, students are often seen as lazy and undisciplined. This narrative is an overgeneralization that can be shifted when more students are working side by side with members of the community in apprenticeships. The media narrative of school can only truly have a counter narrative when schools are baked into the community with programming like apprenticeships.

Empathy can be a two-way street as well. Students rarely see the dedication and non-stop work needed for businesses to survive. They see the products that are sold, but rarely the process to bring them to market. Students and families rarely get a glimpse at marketing, advertising, and customer service, but apprenticeships can bring all this into view and more.

There is a formal apprenticeship program within the Department of Labor. The system consists of a national office, six regional offices, and local offices in each state. The Office of Apprenticeship directly administers the program in 25 states, and delegates some operational authority to state apprenticeship agencies in 25 states and the District of Columbia.

Studies suggest that employers get an average of $1.47 back for every $1 invested in apprenticeships. Iowa, Connecticut, and California have strong state programs that could be used as models for other states, but also for local communities and school districts that see the value of apprenticeships for community partnerships.

Organizations like Jobs for the Future and the Pathways to Prosperity Network both have blueprints for effective homegrown, local apprenticeship programs as well. There are also models on ways to do this in Europe. Many of these countries have built over time strong apprenticeship programs which have become strong career paths for many of their high school students.

Consider these resources as a way to begin the conversation about using the power of apprenticeship to link communities and schools (see information for finding these resources at the end of this chapter):

- *Jobs for the Future*
- *Pathways to Prosperity*
- *The High School Apprenticeship Program*
- *Apprenticeship 2000*

## Advanced Professional Studies

Advanced professional studies, a cousin to the apprenticeship model, is growing in popularity as schools around the country look to prepare students for modern careers. The concepts started with work from Blue Valley, KS, but it has grown into a national network of schools looking to prepare students for the workplace by deeply embedding students in partnerships with current professionals. These programs fast-forward students into their futures, fully immersing them in a professional culture, solving real-world problems, and using industry-standard tools.

This program has come to life in the Affton School District (MO), where they have made connections with a network of local entrepreneurs as well as top local industries. It is this two-fold approach that is helping the school to grow their bench of partnerships. For students, this looks like an opportunity to learn all the parts of the startup culture and practice this through launching their own ideas as well as problem solving for industry through onsite, real-world projects that gives students perspective about the complexity of the modern workplace.

Affton started their work in three areas: engineering design, marketing, and biomedical science. Each of these areas of the advanced professional studies program was identified as an area in the community with the need for a pipeline of workers. The unique feature about Affton's program was the mix of students involved. It included some top students that were choosing this route in lieu of AP courses. It included some students that had tuned out regular school because it didn't seem relevant, and it was diverse in race, gender, and class. This was one of the unique programs, outside of some athletic teams, that brought together this level of diversity under one common vision.

Local advanced professional studies programs continue to rise up with their own local flavor. The Iowa BIG School in Cedar Rapids builds community connection with their unique partnerships and project management software. A program in Waukee, IA, has students working inside of a local architecture firm on design projects for local festivals and the local zoo. The key to success with these programs is an asset-based mentality that sees the students as professionals in training who have something to contribute right now.

Consider these resources as a way to begin the conversation about community engagement through an advanced professional studies model (see information for finding these resources at the end of this chapter):

- *Center for Advanced Professional Studies: Blue Valley*
- *Iowa BIG School*
- *Saint Louis Centers for Advanced Professional Studies*

## Schools of Education

Higher education continues to look for ways to partner that support the communities in which they reside and beyond. This is seen in a variety of programs that schools of education are embarking upon to link students to community resources. The training of teachers is often becoming a secondary mission to surrounding teachers in training with experts, ideas, and resources, so they can carry a network of support into the schools that they will eventually serve.

At the University of Missouri Saint Louis (UMSL), this community mission led to the development of the Collabitat. This unique facility links business mentorships, undergraduate and graduate students, and edupreneurs for the purpose of growing and learning together. By converting an old library into a modern co-working facility, there are opportunities to cross-pollinate ideas in a true spirit of partnership.

The results have been a growing pipeline of innovative school leaders, the breakdown of some traditional cross district barriers, a better sense of the needs of the K–12 space by the higher education instructors, and the launch of a host of local education startups. Over its short existence, the Collabitat has continued to evolved in its mission as it listens to the needs of the community and morphs to meet its needs. This ability to be flexible in mission and iterate has helped to grow powerful partnerships.

School leaders need to continue to look for ways to support the programs that feed teachers into their systems. They need a voice at the higher education table that allows them to both listen and guide the conversation. In a time when we need more and more teachers, we are even more in need of quality modern teachers that can facilitate the deeper learning needed in our classrooms. Engagement in conversations between school districts and schools of education can happen in a number of mechanisms including hosting local professors in schools as well as pop-up learning sessions for school leaders conducted by schools of education professors to unpack research into practice. This level of partnership will provide value for both groups. Even without spaces that facilitate partnerships like the Collabitat, there needs to be greater cocreation and cooperation to meet community needs.

Consider these resources as a way to begin cooperation and partnerships between school districts and higher education as a means to better serve the community (see information for finding these resources at the end of this chapter):

- *Collabitat*
- *Building K-12/Higher Education Partnerships*
- *It Takes Two: The Practical Benefits of K–12 Public Education and Higher Ed Partnerships*
- *The Higher Education–District Partnership Self-Assessment Rubric: An Indicator Tool*

## Intergenerational Learning

We finish with a new idea born from ancient practices. It embraces the circle of life and the wisdom of elders. Intergenerational learning has been a deep part of many cultures over time, but this connected learning has fallen from favor in many places that are less philosophically inclined but more practical. When generations of families live near each other or when groups of individuals gather face-to-face across generations, much intergenerational learning continues, but when these aren't the realities for students, this is a lost opportunity for partnership if it isn't cultivated in a deep way by school districts.

This goes well beyond tutoring, mentors, and reading to students. True intergenerational learning is finding ways to bring the wisdom of life experience into the classroom to help students avoid making the same mistakes as past generations. It means transferring skills and stories to the next generation so that they at least have the opportunity to consider passing them along to their children and beyond. It allows for an appreciation of how technology can ease the demands of work and provides perspective on how many "new" problems have been a part of the fabric of society for a long time.

One unique program in this area can be found in Cleveland, OH. The Intergenerational School blends a council of elders into the daily lives of students. They look for projects and ideas that can shape perspective, build bridges across age barriers, and grow an appreciation for how the years near the end of life can be filled with joy, hope, and challenges.

School districts and educators should consider how honoring often invisible people grows the community at large. There are veterans, heroes, and historians on quiet farms and in assisted living centers that could be a valuable resource to the real-world community-centric work that many desire in the classrooms. In addition, many of these individuals could experience a boost in energy and joy by interacting with the next generation of leaders and citizens in service to their community.

Consider these resources as a way to think about the power of intergenerational learning and its positive community impacts (see information for finding these resources at the end of this chapter):

- *The Intergenerational School*
- *Intergenerational Learning Changes Learning, Changes Lives*
- *European Map of Intergenerational Learning*

Partnership opportunities are robust and available, and it is essential that we begin building them because they are the key to stretching the limited resources of the over 15,000 school districts in the country. Partnerships are essential to a quality future.

It will require some creativity and trust. It will require an ability to see beyond the current structures and systems. It will require leaders that recognize that modern partnerships will mean providing students more freedom in the space that they are learning in. It will require growing teachers that can see and utilize outside resources, and it will require a community understanding of the mission and vision of the district so that schools can become community and communities can become schools.

## References

https://cloudinstitute.org/cloud-efs-standards

https://www.ousd.org/cms/lib07/CA01001176/Centricity/Domain/97/RJ_Strategic_Plan_4_8_09.pdf

http://www.mrhschools.net/userfiles/files/latestheadlines/2011-2012/MRH_Pruitt_Igoe%20Now.pdf

PEW Study available here: http://www.pewsocialtrends.org/2015/05/07/family-size-among-mothers/

https://www.statista.com/statistics/273476/percentage-of-us-population-with-a-social-network-profile/

*Consider these resources as a way to begin the conversation about home visits in your schools—*

- Parent Teacher Home Visits – http://www.pthvp.org/
- Knock Knock, Teacher's Here: The Power Of Home Visits – http://www.npr.org/sections/ed/2015/08/26/434358793/knock-knock-teachers-here-the-power-of-home-visits
- Family Engagement that Works: Parent-Teacher Home Visits – https://www.edutopia.org/blog/family-engagement-works-parent-teacher-home-visits-anne-obrien

*Consider these resources as a way to begin the conversation about arts integration as a philosophy for community engagement—*

- Learning In and Through the Arts – http://www.wholechild education.org/blog/learning-in-and-through-the-arts
- Arts Integration: The Kennedy Center's perspective – https://artsedge.kennedy-center.org/educators/how-to/series/arts-integration/arts-integration
- Teachers and Teaching Artists as Agents of Change – http://press.uchicago.edu/ucp/books/book/distributed/A/bo22229692.html
- ARTS INTEGRATION: New Research on Effective Practice, Sustainability, and the Role of Teachers and Teaching Artists – http://www.aep-arts.org/wp-content/uploads/Arts-Integration-in-Education.pdf

*Consider these resources as a way to begin the conversation about education for sustainability as a philosophy for community engagement—*

- Citizen Science Alliance – https://www.citizensciencealliance.org/
- Children's Environmental Literacy Foundation – http://www.celfeducation.org/who-we-are
- Sustainable Schools Project – http://sustainableschoolsproject.org/education

- Integrated Environmental and Sustainability K–12 Learning Standards – http://www.k12.wa.us/EnvironmentSustainability/Standards/default.aspx

*Consider these resources as a way to begin the conversation about bringing new experts and resources into the school from the larger digital community—*

- Digital Community Engagement Through the Internet – http://www.wicounties.org/uploads/eventmaterials/community-engagement-wca-bh-final.pdf
- Community Partners: Making Student Learning Relevant – https://www.edutopia.org/practice/community-partners-making-student-learning-relevant
- Experts in the Classroom – http://www.scholastic.com/browse/article.jsp?id=3757843

*Consider these resources as a way to begin the conversation about restorative practices can build greater engagement with the community—*

- Restorative Justice in U.S. Schools: A Research Review – https://jprc.wested.org/wp-content/uploads/2016/02/RJ_Literature-Review_20160217.pdf
- Changing School Culture: 5 Schools Practicing Restorative Justice – http://blackorganizingproject.org/changing-school-culture-5-schools-practicing-restorative-justice/
- Videos & Films on Restorative Practices in Schools – http://restorativesolutions.us/videos-on-restorative-practices-in-schools
- Restorative Response to Ferguson, NYC, Cleveland – http://peacealliance.org/restorative-response-to-ferguson-nyc-cleveland/
- Reducing Harms to Boys and Young Men of Color from Criminal Justice System Involvement – http://www.urban.org/sites/default/files/publication/39551/2000095-Reducing-Harms-to-Boys-and-Young-Men-of-Color-from-Criminal-Justice-System-Involvement.pdf

*Consider these resources as a way to begin the conversation about using the design of the civic and business communities to showcase how change is possible—*

- Center for Communities by Design – https://www.aia.org/pages/2891-center-for-communities-by-design
- Community By Design: New Urbanism for Suburbs and Small Communities – https://www.amazon.com/Community-Design-Urbanism-Suburbs-Communities/dp/007134523X
- Resources for Building Community Partnerships – https://www.edutopia.org/article/community-business-partnerships-resources
- A How-to Guide for School-Business Partnerships – http://www.nhscholars.org/School-Business%20How_to_Guide.pdf
- Toolkit for Building Partnerships between Schools and Businesses or Organizations across South Washington County Schools – http://www.sowashco.org/files/community/partnerships/Toolkit.pdf

*Consider these resources as a way to begin the conversation about using power of apprenticeship to link communities and schools—*

- Jobs for the Future – http://www.jff.org/
- Pathways to Prosperity – http://www.jff.org/initiatives/pathways-prosperity-network
- The High School Apprenticeship Program – http://www.usaeop.com/programs/apprenticeships/hsap/
- Apprenticeship 2000 – http://apprenticeship2000.com/zwp/

*Consider these resources as a way to begin the conversation about community engagement through an advanced professional studies model—*

- Center for Advanced Professional Studies- Blue Valley – http://bvcaps.yourcapsnetwork.org/
- Iowa BIG School – https://www.iowabig.org/
- Saint Louis Centers for Advanced Professional Studies – https://stlcaps.yourcapsnetwork.org/

*Consider these resources as a way to begin cooperation and partner-ships between school districts and higher education as a means to better serve the community—*

- Collabitat – http://collabitat.umsl.edu/
- Building K-12/ Higher Education Partnerships – https:// compact.org/resource-posts/building-k-12higher-education-partnerships/
- It Takes Two: The Practical Benefits of K-12 Public Education and Higher Ed Partnerships – https://www.edsurge.com/news/2016-04-21-it-takes-two-the-practical-benefits-of-k-12-public-educa-tion-and-higher-ed-partnerships
- The Higher Education– District Partnership Self-Assessment Rubric: An Indicator Tool – http://www.annenberginstitute.org/ sites/default/files/product/814/files/HigherEducationRubric.pdf

*Consider these resources as a way to think about the power of inter-generational learning and its positive community impacts—*

- The Intergenerational School – http://tisonline.org/
- Intergenerational Learning Changes Learning, Changes Lives – https:// www.edutopia.org/blog/intergenerational-learning-brendan-okeefe
- European Map of Intergenerational Learning – http://www.emil-network.eu/what-is-intergenerational-learning/

# 10

# Changing the Narrative

## Joe Sanfelippo

This chapter is dedicated to all the young people who go out of their way to help friends dealing with depression or suicidal thoughts. Thanks for showing you care—it makes a difference!

I was 8 years old and I remember it like it happened yesterday. My parents drove me up to the front of the brand new building. It was gorgeous. The windows were incredibly clean. The flowers leading up to the door were perfect. My mom grabbed my hand and we walked through the parking lot together. She told me it was going to be OK and she understood how I was feeling because it wasn't her favorite place as a kid either.

We walked into the building and even the smells reminded me of the last time I had entered. The pit in my stomach was real. I knew exactly how the day was going to go. I was going to be told I needed to do things differently and at one point someone would sit down with my mom and tell her what had to change at home to make things better.

As we waited in the front office I thought about all the times I had been there in the past. They all shaped the way I was feeling at that moment, and that feeling wasn't great. Minutes seemed like hours. I started to get anxious, could feel my palms sweating profusely, and my heart started to race. It was almost time.

I just wanted to hide. I kept thinking of what I could have done to make what was going to happen next more manageable.

The door from the waiting area started to open slowly, and it was time. A very friendly woman opened the door with a bright smile and a skip in her step. It was clearly not what I needed at that point. She looked at my mom, then looked at me, and said, "Dr. Craig will see you now."

It was the first of two dental appointments that month. My parents used to make both appointments for me every six months—one for the cleaning and one to get the inevitable cavities filled. It was easier to schedule both at the same time knowing they would happen. Needless to say, every walk into a dentist's office since has been fraught with feelings of early morning appointments that ended in one side of my face being numb and food tasting like metal for a day. It's not a great feeling, but I have to acknowledge that it's real.

Advances in dental technology have made going to the dentist a very different experience. The people who work in the dental office are fantastic. They are welcoming, knowledgeable, and I believe they have my best interest in mind. Having said that, I still get an awkward feeling in my stomach as I walk through the parking lot to the door. There are a number of factors that contribute to that feeling. Not having breakfast and "cramming" for the appointment by brushing my teeth an extra 15 minutes, just to make sure they are as clean as possible, certainly contribute to the feeling I have walking into the building, but past experience, frequency, and current state of mind all play a role in how I enter that building.

Walking into schools should not feel like a long walk to the dentist chair, but we have to understand that everyone walking into our building may not feel like it is the best experience in the world. The reality is that everyone had a different experience in school and, like it or not, those experiences shape the attitude that our public has when it walks through the hallways. The story doesn't change until we acknowledge that it's real; we need to be intentional about changing the narrative, and build momentum for the next generation of students, teachers, and community members to ensure that the stories reflect what is happening in that space.

I love walking into our school every day, but I have to understand that a number of people do not have that same sense of comfort. My guess is that people who worked in that dentist's office don't have the same feeling of my visits. I have to think they felt like the dental office was a good place to work and the mission they had to make their clients' smiles brighter was at the heart of every move. They probably felt like they were making a difference. They probably felt like smiling and adding a skip to their step would make everyone feel like it was a place they wanted to be. It wasn't their fault that I felt the way I did.

Educators, look around and see who is leading students. Likely, the majority of teachers in your building had a relatively good experience in school. People don't choose to spend their careers in a place where they had a bad experience. The experiences that our staff members had in school are not always the same as those of the parents who send their most prized possessions to us every day. The narrative needs to be changed. This is how we do it.

## It Starts With Us

Some believe that we chose this profession, others believe it chose us. Whatever you believe got you to the place where you have the opportunity to inspire doesn't mean nearly as much as what you do now that you have that platform. We can be our own worst enemy at times. First and foremost, we often believe that we are a service organization and therefore promoting the work done in our area seems a bit braggadocian. It doesn't fit who we are. That needs to change.

The work educators are doing across the country is astounding. Thinking about this rationally for a second. The OECD estimates class sizes in their member organizations at 24.1. According to the Pew Research Center (PEW, 2015), the average mother has 2.4 children. So, in our infinite wisdom as educators, we decided to put 21.7 more bodies in one room and have you educate them. Some that had breakfast, some that had none. Some that got a brother or sister ready for school, some that wish they had a sibling to share their day with. Some that want more hugs at home, some that have adults who hang on every breath they take. They all come to one place and we expect you to move them . . . and you do it. You do it. We can write words upon words about how to change the narrative or the leadership or the mental health process or assessment, but the one thing that doesn't change is your ability to make it happen. You are the change agent. You are where we need to start. You have more value than you can possibly imagine, and others need to know what your colleagues already know: the work that happens in your space is astounding. It's time to tell someone about it.

As a first-year principal I walked around our school looking for things that I needed to correct. From students walking on the wrong side of the hallway to not having a pass to get from one part of the building the other. I defaulted to no. In continuously looking at the things that were going wrong in school, I was closing my mind to all of the wonderful things that were happening in that space. I didn't realize the impact I was having on our school until kids started to look away when they walked down our hallways. I would smile as they were walking where they were asked to walk or had the pass they needed to get to where they were going, but I didn't say anything. The only time I talked to them was when I needed to make a correction. I was crushing the culture of the building without saying a word. The change came when I started to think about the impact of our first contact.

## First Contact

There are feelings in schools . . . we have all had them. When visiting other schools I think you can get a pretty good indication of the environment upon entering the building. The first contact—from secretarial help, to seeing a teacher in the hallway, to a custodian in the entrance—can shape the relationships we have with parents. We need to trust our staff to engage the public when they enter our building. As leaders in the building it is imperative that we relay the importance of the first contact with parents to our staff members. When parents enter the building the default feeling can be how they felt as a kid. If our first contact is welcoming, we can make them feel like they are a part of something bigger than dropping off in the morning and picking up at the end of the day.

*Listen*—People want to be heard. Often behind the volume and vigor of parent complaints is a message. Sometimes we can't find the message through the tone, but it is there and is always an opportunity to get better. I am not advocating that we put all suggestions or complaints into action, but we do need to hear where they are coming from and honestly reflect on what we are doing. My first inclination as an educator was to defend. When I had that mindset I gave up the listening to instead focus on crafting the response in my head. In essence, I had entered a battle that I was not going to win, but somewhere in my head I felt like I had to be right. Developing trust in your group isn't about always being right and if that is the mentality, true trust will never occur.

*Call*—We call parents within three days of the start of the year. The first call to parents can be short, but has to be positive. Our administrators make positive calls (we set the goal at four per week) to parents regarding *anything* a student is doing well at school. The power of these calls has been fantastic. The four calls take 30 minutes every week . . . at the most. The idea of first contact doesn't need to be relegated to the physical school building. If our first contact is positive, regardless of venue, we will be in a better spot. When making the calls, we cite the specific action that was positive. The easy way is to call a person and tell them that their child is awesome. News flash: they already know that. They don't need you to tell them that their child is awesome; they need you to tell them why. Take a look at the difference in these two phone calls:

> "Hi Andrea, this is Dr. Sanfelippo from school. I just wanted to let you know that Aidan is awesome. He really is. I truly enjoy being around him."

This call gets Andrea to smile. It makes her feel good that someone is acknowledging she has an awesome kid, but that joy is only going to last for a little while. Here is another example:

> "Hi Andrea, this is Dr. Sanfelippo from school. I wanted to let you know that I just left a 3rd grade classroom

and had a chance to see Aidan reading to a 3rd grade student. First and foremost, the idea that a 16-year-old would take time out of his day to spend reading with a 3rd grader was fantastic. The thing that got me, though, was as he was reading to her, she looked up at him like he was a god. She hung on every word he said and he read with a passion that spoke to me. When he asked her questions about the story, the look on her face told me she felt like she was the only person in the entire world. That was incredibly special for me to see. Clearly along the way you have instilled the idea that focusing on the person in front of you is important and makes them feel valued. I just wanted to say thank you. My day is a lot better because of the last 20 minutes."

Two things to remember about that conversation. First, don't hang up right away. The silence is Andrea holding back tears on the other end of the phone. Parenting is hard and they don't always get the positive feedback from others because they are just trying to keep their heads above water. Give Andrea a minute to gather her thoughts and respond. Second, take the next step in this journey by asking if you can share that story with others on your social media feeds. Sharing a story like that, with a visual, hits the emotion of your community. When you post it, see how long it takes for Andrea to share that story on her page and tag everyone in her family to it. What if we lived in a world where people were waiting at their computer or phone for something from the school district so they could share it with the world? We have that capability. It's time to get social.

## Building Momentum Through Social Channels

The connections made in schools are astounding, but often we are the only people who get to relish that joy. In the previous example Andrea is not only feeling good about the work Aidan is doing in school; she is feeling good about the work she has done at home to get Aidan to that point. The other positive derived from the phone call is the impact of how Andrea views the caller. If Dr. Sanfelippo is an administrator, Andrea knows that he doesn't spend his days locked behind a closed door. She knows he is in classrooms connected to students, and she will tell that story. If Dr. Sanfelippo is the teacher Andrea knows that he took the time to connect with her and, more importantly, he is paying attention to her child. Both have a tremendous impact on Andrea's perception of the school. Changing the narrative with people in your school tends to be much easier than those who are outside of it, simply because you have more opportunities on a daily basis. Making calls and connections to people in the building helps build the momentum for those you see on a regular basis, but it doesn't address the issue that 80% of the people in your community do not have kids in school. We want them all to be on the journey with us, on their terms, not ours. People want to connect, but they want to do it on a schedule that fits them. We are completely OK with that because at the end of the day it is not about the time of the connection, but whether it happens. Our goal is to bring everyone together with an accurate picture of the amazing work our kids and teachers do on a daily basis.

We look at time as a commodity, one that we can harness but not control. Parents and community members will engage in what we do if we give them the opportunity, but do not force the issue of time on them. We take an ABC approach to connecting to our community to help change the narrative of our school: We find our Audience, Build our brand, and Celebrate kids.

## Find Your AUDIENCE

According to statista.com (Statista, n.d.), 81% of adults have a social media profile of some kind in 2017. As a district we needed to find where those profiles lived. After surveying our community we found that adults preferred Facebook, students preferred Instagram, and alumni preferred Twitter. So, that is where we engage socially. We don't have to be present in every social media platform, just the platforms that are relevant to our people. Once we found where people lived, we started engaging them online through social media contests such as:

## Throwback Thursdays

Connecting to the community means valuing the world they lived in before they left school. We honor tradition by making those who came before us proud. Part of that is taking them along on the journey. Posting pictures from years gone by to a current social media platform helps bridge the past to the present. All those pictures come with a story. Start the story on the platform and then allow people to contribute to it. A community telling a story is a powerful connection tool and celebrates everyone involved.

## What Is the Vision?

During the first two weeks after we started our social media presence the response was not overwhelming. We had a few people follow our feeds on Twitter and Facebook, but the vast majority of people were not aware of our social media presence. That changes substantially when we started to have conversations about school, rather than posting what was happening. On a warm night in 2011 we engaged in our first interactive post on Facebook. The post was simple: "The first 5 people to find Dr. Sanfelippo at the football game tonight and tell him the vision of Fall Creek Schools will receive t-shirts." The response was phenomenal. As I walked into the game I saw kids running from across the field as fast as their little legs would carry them. They screamed, "We're a community that works, learns, and succeeds together!" I handed out t-shirts to the first five people and had a wonderful time at the game, feeling great about the response to the post. The following week we went through the same process. As I entered the game something different happened. Again, the kids came running as fast as they could, but I looked behind the kids and couldn't believe what I saw. The adults were sprinting to get in front of the kids and they were screaming as they ran, "We're a community that works, learns, and succeeds together!" People often want to be connected to a greater entity. When we are all carrying the flag it becomes lighter and our voice is much louder.

## Build Your BRAND

The term *brand* can definitely have a negative connotation, but we believe it is what people say about you when you are not there. Promoting the positives helps shape the narrative. Building our brand through a message or social media hashtag has helped us share the work of our kids in multiple areas. Putting the hashtag on apparel and giving it to the community at events built a tremendous amount of momentum for our district. We also added a "Where in the World Is Fall Creek Pride" virtual map, and told our community to take pictures in their Cricket gear on vacation so we can spread the message. It has allowed us to show off a #gocrickets item in all 50 states and beyond. We have tried to turn those Go Crickets moments into a Go Crickets movement and that movement makes our group feel like they can accomplish anything.

### Leverage the Voice

Six of our teachers attended a conference in Orlando, Florida, to present on a professional growth that put the ownership of learning on our staff. They developed the whole model, created ownership capacity with our teachers, and they were now being recognized as a District of Innovation by the International Center for Leadership in Education. They were excited to be there and share their story with the world. What they were not prepared for was the response from those who attended the conference. As they walked through hallways and attended sessions, donning their Fall Creek t-shirts and backpacks, people at the conference would yell "Go Crickets!" at them on a regular basis. At first they were a little alarmed, but after it happened a few times I saw one turn to a colleague, smile, and say, "They know us." The sense of pride they all felt at that moment helped me understand that this movement was about much more than a mascot or a saying. It was about value, and on that day our people were valued. They started to send messages to their colleagues and tell them what was happening. When they returned to the school district we asked them to do their presentation for the board of education. As they finished their presentation one of the board members asked how their trip went. One member of the team looked at her colleagues, then at me, then to the board member, and said, "We felt like rock stars."

## CELEBRATE Kids

The work done in our schools is amazing if you think about it. We educate *all* kids, we move them academically and emotionally, we provide a safe haven for those who need it, and celebrating that work should be at the forefront of what we do as school systems. As a board, we set a goal of 7–10 non-athletic positive posts per week. Our community knows that the space is to celebrate and we want everyone to join us on the journey.

We provide the opportunity to connect and through that connection we develop a great deal of social capital with the people in our world. That social capital is pivotal for trust. A picture, video, or post can have a profound impact on emotions. The world has belonged, and will always belong, to the storytellers.

## Development of Social Capital

Winter weather in Wisconsin can get a bit crazy. The snow, wind, and cold often impact the drive to and from school. Bus routes can often be delayed in that process. When those delays happen we try to do everything we can to make sure parents are alerted to adjustments in the pick up/drop off schedule. We often send out an email, post to our social media accounts, text message, and sometimes autocall to make sure everyone knows and there are not students waiting outside in the inclement weather. In my first superintendent year in Fall Creek I wanted to let the community know that one of our bus routes was going to be delayed. So, as I have done hundreds of times before, I emailed everyone on the school contact list. The intent was to construct a quick email and get it out as soon as possible. I started the email with "Hello everyone" and then went on to let everyone know that the bus was going to be late. In my quest to get the email out quickly I had forgotten the "o" in "Hello." Though it wasn't a big mistake, the response from the community could have been negative if we hadn't built social capital leading up to that point. Every post, conversation, and connection either build or detract from your social capital. We try to be very cognizant of the momentum we are building through all our posts. The balance in our community has been 7–10 non-athletic positive posts per week. That gives us a social presence, yet doesn't overwhelm the feeds of those you want to connect with throughout the year.

## What Happens When Things Go Wrong?

Our family loves to travel. We talk, laugh, and see things through our journeys that inspire and make us think. On one of our recent trips we got a flat tire. It took time to fix and definitely had an impact on the next part of the trip. In the grand scheme of things it wasn't a big deal. We still got to where we were going and had fun along the way. When we got the flat tire we didn't decide to shut everything down and stop the trip. We just fixed it and moved on. At some point on the changing-the-narrative journey you are going to come across a flat tire. Someone will reply to a post on your social media pages with a negative comment or call your school out for something that happened. Your reaction to that instance will definitely impact how long it lasts. We always do two things with negative social media replies. The first is to address the issue with a consistent statement on the page. Ours reads: "I'm sorry you are feeling this way. I'd love to talk to you about it. Please give me a call and we can talk about it, but this is not the place where we have those discussions." The second thing is to make it a point to get into more classrooms and post an inordinate amount of positive stories to bury the negative comment. What we have found is that people don't go to our

Facebook page to see what is happening. They go to their page to see the latest posts.

## Connecting Your Staff

Events evoke emotion. The game you went to, the motivational speaker you cheered with, and the book that made you want to look at your classroom differently. Often we see something that changes our social norm and gets us excited about doing things better. However, we are then thrown back into the normal day-to-day operation of what school is and the farther we get from the event the harder it is to change the current practice. We use the 72-hour rule of implementation. When our staff learns something new—be it a resource tool or pedagogical practice—we ask them to attempt to use it within 72 hours of the learning event. That gives them a few days to find a way to move it into what they are currently doing, but not so far out that the impact of the emotion goes away. The vast majority of influence for staff in our building to use social media as a way to build momentum came from teacher colleagues, not administration. When we first started using the platforms there were a number of people who viewed it as one more thing on an already full plate of duties throughout the day. Being cognizant of that thought, it was truly important for us as an administrative team to provide a few things to everyone to help move them forward. We viewed time, resource, and opportunity as a way to do that.

*Time*—Get your staff connected to a social media platform that meets the need of your school community. Twitter, Instagram, and/or review online blogs or webinars that spark their interest. Many of the platforms are already being used by staff members for social reasons. Give them time to explore the space and see if they can find one resource that can help them in a professional manner. We tend to "over-agenda" a number of days throughout the year. Trading a meeting for a chance to explore will help them know you value their time. At some point the conversation about time will come up when discussing how we get the word out to people who don't live in that world daily.

Giving people time in their day to explore how social media platforms can be used to tell stories and for professional gain is important as they have to see value in the why.

*Resource*—Record (or find) videos on how to use social media professionally to promote the work happening in your space. Send them out in a medium that they currently use, probably email. This way they don't have to get out of their comfort zone to start the process, which is where we lose a number of people. Provide multiple resources that could be used and always provide the "why" and "how" they could benefit from the tool. Develop a resource page that has links helping people navigate the tools. Take it a step further and use a Twitter hashtag that links the learning to an online platform so more people can contribute. As the leader in your organization, be sure to contribute to both the learning and celebration of student work. It models the way and shows your vulnerability. This will empower your staff to take risks when it comes to sharing their space.

*Opportunity*—Continue the conversations as the year goes on. Use the social media platforms to hold impromptu staff meetings. Using the platforms creates a credibility that will be needed when the middle of the year comes and many are in survival mode. It also helps the group become more comfortable with the tools so the "I don't have enough time for this" mentality is alleviated a bit. As the comfort level rises, the use of the tools will rise. Having said that, the tools will change, so providing the opportunity to be comfortable with being uncomfortable will model a process that will last when new platforms become available.

## Never Give Up the Opportunity to Say Something Great About Your School

We tend to talk about hope a lot. We have hope that the narrative of our schools will change. We hope that people will tell great stories about the time they spent in our buildings. We hope that when those that did not have a great experience provide their opinion someone will step in and talk about the positive aspect of their own experience. Hope is great and we all need hope, but hope doesn't change narratives, action does. We need to make a commitment to the kids, colleagues, and community members that put their heart and soul into the work to make the world a better place. I truly and honestly believe that people want to celebrate the work that happens in schools, I just don't know if they have the context to do so. Our job is to provide the context and if we remain unapologetically optimistic about the work done in schools the narrative will change. If we never give up the opportunity to say something great about the people who work with our kids and the work that those kids do, the narrative will change. If we provide a sense of pride and understanding that our voice is stronger together, the narrative will change. The world belongs to the storytellers and it is time to write ours.

# Afterword

## Changing the Way We Think About Collaboration

### Jimmy Casas

A few weeks ago I was listening to a podcast on school leadership when I heard a guest share his views with the host on the topic of collaborative leadership. One particular comment caught my attention. He shared that if school leaders are to be successful, they must expect their teachers to work collaboratively in teams. Moreover, he went on to say that schools which have teachers operating independently of each other are more likely to fail than those of their counterparts.

His comments made me pause and ask the question, "Does it have to be either-or?" Are there not times in our work as educators that a certain situation cannot demand both? It's as though we have stigmatized those who at times prefer to work alone to the point we now hesitate to do so for fear of being viewed as an individual rather than as a team player. Our profession is often critical of those who want to work independently as though somehow these individuals are isolating themselves from others in exchange for collegial discourse. On the contrary, there is a difference between working independently and working in isolation. When I think of working independently, I think of learners still being influenced by outside sources, often leading to a broader perspective and deeper understanding.

As a young child, I would often lie in bed, look up, and see war planes flying above me. I was 10 years old at the time and my older brother and I had decorated the bedroom we shared with model airplanes. War planes to be exact. Coming down from the ceiling were Tomcats, twin-engine Hornets and even B-52 bombers, suspended in mid-air, taped with kite string and masking tape. I could tell by the decals whether they were American planes or if they were enemy fighter planes belonging to the Germans or Japanese. Once a month my dad would take us to the local hobby shop and purchase a model plane for each of us. We would get home and immediately tear open our boxes with excitement, get out the instructions and begin to lay out the parts one by one on opposite sides of the dining room table, neither one us wanting the other to see our work until the plane had been completely constructed. We would work independently, delicately putting a drop of model glue on each part as we assembled our planes with pride. But it was not only pride that drove us, but the competitive nature of who could build their plane the fastest, make the propeller spin, pull the lever and have the bombs drop, make the wheels rotate on takeoff, and put the decals on without tearing them. Quality counted too. And that is where I needed my brother the most when it came to assembling my plane. It was not uncommon for me to misread the instructions and glue a part that was not meant to be glued. Or worse yet, finish a section and have parts left over. Needless to say, it was in these moments that my brother would laugh or tease me about messing up and then frustration would set in and cause me to want to give up. But he never let me. Instead, he would slide over to my side of the table, sit down next to me, and begin to guide me through step by step until I was ready to venture off on my own again. And just like that, I would go back at it again, working independently—and then collaboratively again whenever I needed his help.

Ironically, what I observed over the course of the two days in Philadelphia as the authors of this book came together to write wasn't much different. I saw professional educators given a task, timeline, and clear instructions before eagerly beginning to work. Some authors chose to leave the premises, venturing off to tackle their writing assignment head on. Other writers stayed in the conference room while a few others wandered to the lobby, preferring a soft sofa chair or high-top table to inspire their thinking. Interestingly, most selected to put on headphones or earbuds and bop to their favorite tunes in order to drown out the noise around them. Over the next few hours, I got a first-hand glimpse into what learning looks like for different people. Some chose to work alone in a corner away from peers while others enjoyed the comfort of someone sitting next to them. Some were able to focus for what seemed like hours while others either checked their text messages or posted items on their social media pages as though their brains needed a break from the added stress of a short timeline. Two others would get up and move around every 10–15 minutes as though sitting still for any length of time seemed an impossible task. Every now and then I could see the frustration on an author's face and sense self-doubt beginning to take over as they moved to sidle up next to someone, looking for a new set of eyes and ears to collect a fresh idea to help them regroup and continue writing. During the time they worked together they worked, well, collaboratively. But each time this collaboration looked different. When it appeared as though they had exhausted their moments of independence, they would revert back to working collaboratively and vice versa, moving back and forth effortlessly, depending on what their brains needed in that moment. In other words, sometimes they just needed to refresh their experiences.

They worked, it seemed, as independent collaborators. Independent in one moment, yet collaborative in the next moment. They combined the best of both methods to meet their needs when the time called for it. Much like, I would suspect, we believe good teaching looks like in the classroom when we ask teachers to differentiate for the variety of learner differences they encounter on a daily basis. After all, don't we expect our teachers to consider the learning environment for students, creating flexible learning spaces for them that are conducive to their learning styles, thus allowing them to work as independent collaborators, whether it be working alone, with partners or in small or large groups in order to personalize their learning?

Most educators would probably agree that all of us learn differently. Whether you are a teacher, counselor, secretary, curriculum director or principal, I don't think any of us is that different when it comes to wanting to accomplish an assignment, a task, or a project successfully. We can be our own worst critics. I think it is because we are constantly under scrutiny, often being reminded when we fail to meet certain expectations and goals. Sometimes our outcomes fall short, even when our processes are solid. Whether we are working in content or grade level teams, partnering with instructional coaches, doing teacher exchanges with other school districts, or taking advantage of the digital tools available to us in order to connect with other educators around the country, I would argue that in the end, regardless of whether you are a student or an educator, there is a place for both the way "I do it" and the way "we do it." What is important is that we just don't talk about collaboration, but we live it, both independently and collectively. I applaud the authors of this important book for thinking differently about how we view education and how we write about our thinking. They model the way for others with this collaborative effort and observing them working on this project has changed the way I think about collaboration.